PLAYERS AT WORK

PLAYERS AT WORK

ACTING *according to* THE ACTORS

BY MORTON EUSTIS

With a chapter on the Singing Actor

BY LOTTE LEHMANN

Essay Index Reprint Series

BOOKS FOR LIBRARIES PRESS, INC.
FREEPORT, NEW YORK

First published 1937
Reprinted 1967

PRINTED IN THE UNITED STATES OF AMERICA

Contents

Illustrations

Prologue

EVER since Shakespeare — assuming the mantle of Hamlet, Prince of Denmark — penned what is probably the most widely quoted critique on the art of acting, the technique of the player in the theatre has been subjected to every known form of literary analysis and review. Critics and scholars, essayists and poets have torn passions to tatters extolling, or condemning actors and theories of acting. Daily and Sundays, in the world's theatrical centres, the mirror of acting has been held up to every conceivable type of nature and of art, without finding the final answer to the question: 'What is acting?'

The actors alone, in all the controversy, have remained comparatively silent and aloof. Coquelin and Henry Irving, to be sure, did carry on a brilliant and delightful discussion on the relative importance of intellect and emotion in the actor's art. Fanny Kemble, William Gillette and a few others have made sporadic appearances in the periodicals of their time. But, for the most part, the world's players, following Hamlet's ad-

vice, have gone about their business, suiting the action
to the word, the word to the action on the stage.

The reason for their muteness on a subject concerning
them deeply, lies not alone in natural reticence but in
the temperament and the special medium of expression
which are the actor's heritage. The player's whole approach to art, and even to life itself, is one of interpretation. In the theatre, he creates life out of the rib of a
playwright's imagination. Off the stage, he relates life,
as he sees and feels it, to life as it must be seen, felt,
recreated on the boards. His natural medium of expression is movement, gesture, a dramatist's speech. His
own vocabulary — like his personality and physique —
belongs to the playwright. And though, occasionally, a
generous providence may add the gift of literary expression to other natural endowments, as with Coquelin, and
with Mme. Lotte Lehmann and with Stanislavski, more
often than not, the actor who is able to express himself
freely in his *own* words is unable to translate a dramatist's words into living action on a stage.

Leonard Merrick's actress, Naomi Knight, is an ad-
mirable case in point. If Miss Knight could emerge from
between the still covers of *The Position of Peggy Har-
per*, she could unquestionably recount the secrets of
acting far more clearly than any actor playing on Broadway, or anywhere else. No one could tell you more accurately the exact point where technique blended into
art, where movement, emotion, gesture, pitch of voice,
rhythm and tempo, timing — what you will — fused into

something timeless. The only thing, in point of fact, that she did not know about acting (a detail worthy of mention only to adorn a tale and not to point a moral) was how to put her knowledge into practice when she stepped into the glare of the footlights. 'The woman whose dramatic intelligence was so acute in the parlor,' her creator avers, 'displayed not the least touch of inspiration on the stage. . . . She knew as much about the meaning of the part as the man who had written it, but the lines, when she spoke them, made no impression whatever.' No matter. She was a great dressing-room actress. She knew the answers to all the questions. Would that she were alive today!

Actors who know how to act, however, like any craftsmen who can apply their technique successfully to their art, must have a better fundamental understanding of the 'manner of their artistic execution, the part of their artistic work that is reducible to formula' (to follow the Oxford Dictionary's definition of technique) than any layman. They may be unable, themselves, to express this knowledge on paper; they may not enact the role of analyst to an interpreter as smoothly, as fluently or as articulately as they perform on a stage; they may pretend that it is impossible to fathom the method of an actor's achievement, or suggest that technique is an instrument that defies analysis. Still and all, an actor's own appraisal of an actor's own problems — if translated into layman's terms — ought to be at least as illuminating as the comments of the dressing-room *artiste* even if it fails to reveal the final 'how's and why's, the when's and if's' of acting.

The studies that follow are a reporter's attempt to make such a translation of the ideas and opinions of a few contemporary actors on their methods of work and performance. The articles make no pretense at being anything but factual reports; whatever value they may possess rests on the fact that they are practical, rather than theoretical records of the way in which actors attack their roles. The material was collected by seeing the actors, putting a list of leading questions before them, and encouraging them to comment on the points raised by the questions. Their comments were then correlated into articles; the articles were submitted to the actors for consideration and approval.

Awaiting the moment, then, when Mr. Merrick's heroine emerges from her bookish limbo to jot down, once and for all, the whole truth about the technique of performance, we present Helen Hayes, Alfred Lunt and Lynn Fontanne, Nazimova, Katharine Cornell, Ina Claire, Burgess Meredith, Fred Astaire and Lotte Lehmann — performers all of them, who *can* act — to tell their part of the tale.

PLAYERS AT WORK

1. Helen Hayes

HELEN HAYES' first conception of a play, and of her own role in it, is entirely objective. Her initial concern is with the play in relation to itself. She analyzes the structure of the drama — the plot, the motivation. She studies all the parts, tries to acquire a clear picture of the characters — 'what they look like, what they are thinking of, what their relationship is to one another, the quality of their personalities'. Once this first reading has convinced her that the play tells a story in the language of the theatre which seems worth telling, she reads the script again — quickly, this time — concentrating on the role that would be hers, assuring herself that the part is a good one, and, more important, that she likes it. Then she makes her decision.

Up to this point she has not considered the role in terms of Helen Hayes acting the part on the stage. Rather, she has thought of the character as a person quite apart from herself, a flesh and blood woman living, not acting, in the world conceived by the dramatist. When she visualizes her making a gesture, speaking a

15

line, it is always as an individual, never as an actress. Even, much later, when the contracts are signed and press releases sent out announcing her engagement in the play, she does not allow herself, consciously at least, to project herself as an actress into the role. She studies the part for days or weeks until a complete picture of the character, as a character, is focused in her mind. When she feels that she knows the person as well as herself, and preferably better, when, in her mind's eye, she can see the character as clearly as if she held a photograph of the woman before her eyes, then she starts to consider the problem of relating Helen Hayes, the woman and the actress, to the conception she has formed.

This is where technique enters the scene. It is also the point at which Miss Hayes begins to interlard simple, declarative statements about methods and means with notes of interrogation; to pause, to hesitate, to make assurance far less sure. For Miss Hayes is an ardent champion of the credo: 'Deliver us from all dressing-room theories of acting!' She does not believe any actor can describe exactly how he acts. Nor does she think that scholarly essays on the subject by those who cannot act add much to the sum total of knowledge about acting, a viewpoint all actors seem to share. An actor, she feels, creates a part out of instinct, imagination and technique. How these qualities are blended — how much of one, how little of the other, contributes to an interpretation — even the actor cannot always tell. For the manner in which he approaches a part and adapts him-

HELEN HAYES
in *Mary of Scotland* – 1933

HELEN HAYES
in *Victoria Regina* – 1936

self to it depends not only upon his conception of a given role, but upon his physique, his personality, his experience and range; upon the hundred and one elements of character and qualities of acting that differentiate an actor from a puppet.

Ever since Miss Hayes stepped before the footlights of the National Theatre in Washington in 1908 to make her professional debut in *The Babes in the Woods* (she was then six years old), it has been her 'sweet dream' that she submerge her own personality completely in each role she played; that her impersonation of Pollyanna in 1918, for instance, enabled the audience to envisage Pollyanna instead of Helen Hayes; that the same happy truth applied to the small parts which led up to Shaw's Cleopatra and Barrie's Maggie Wylie in 1925 and '26, and to the roles in *Coquette, Mr. Gilhooley,* and *The Good Fairy* which led in turn to a successful film career and a triumphant return to the stage as Mary Stuart in Maxwell Anderson's *Mary of Scotland.* Surveying the record from the vantage point of her role as England's Queen in *Victoria Regina* — the greatest *tour de force* of acting she will probably ever be called upon to perform — Miss Hayes admits that her aim to subjugate Helen Hayes, the person, to the character she plays has probably been achieved but rarely in the eyes of her audience. Nevertheless, as far as *she* is concerned, she believes firmly, 'most of the time', that she succeeds in her intention.

From the moment she begins to weigh the part in

terms of acting and a stage — long before rehearsals —
until the last night of the play's run, Miss Hayes keeps
always in front of her the mental vision of the woman
she is going to portray, and tries never, in rehearsal
or during a performance, to visualize herself made up
as the woman. This by no means implies that she is not
always fully conscious of the fact that she is acting a part.
But it is essential to her — 'another actor may have an
entirely different approach' — if she is to give anything
but a mechanical performance, if she is to project across
the footlights the phantasy of a character other than her
own, that the right illusion of the part should be constantly in the forefront of her own mind. The moment
that she became more aware of Helen Hayes playing
the part of Mary Stuart than of Mary Stuart portrayed
by Helen Hayes — fine as the distinction is — the audience would lose the sense that she was a real character.

'Half the actor's battle is won,' Miss Hayes believes,
'once a clear picture of the character is firmly engraved
in his senses.' Knowing the person, the player will recognize, almost instinctively, the characteristic gesture,
the expression, the tone of voice consistent with a given
situation, and he will use whatever tools prove most
serviceable to him at the moment — 'will-power, imagination, technique' — to project these elements of character. In *Mary of Scotland* Miss Hayes had to battle
against every conceivable handicap, physical and mental,
in the struggle to adapt herself to the role. Her conception of Mary Stuart — 'like almost everyone else's' —

was of a woman completely removed from Helen Hayes — 'tall, dark, a sombre, brooding creature, a dominant, magnetic personality, iron willed'. How transform Helen Hayes — very short, slight, light-haired, more like Maggie Wylie than Mary Stuart in real life — into the image of Scotland's tragic Queen? Technique could give the movement, the gesture, the carriage to express the dignity and force of Mary's regal presence. With long endeavor, technique could even master the difficulties of diction (almost the hardest element in the play for Miss Hayes to master. It was her first attempt at the romantic, poetic school of acting. It needed a diction entirely removed from naturalism, a control of the breath and an ability to support it for the duration of a phrase which she had never required before). Make-up could alter the expression, the color of the hair; costumes could reclothe, even reshape the body. But make-up and costume could produce only a superficial likeness to a conventional and lifeless portrait. Technique could only supply the externals of character and relate them — brilliantly, if the technique was brilliant — to the theatre. Something more was needed to give this figure life, to make it three-dimensional.

What that something was, Miss Hayes does not attempt to say. She wore slightly higher heels during the performance of *Mary of Scotland*. But heels, alone, could not have made her look so much taller than in previous roles. 'Size, like character,' she believes, 'is mental. You can make yourself taller on the stage. You can make the audience see, or think they see, what isn't there. How, I don't quite know. Magic, perhaps, plus technique.' Often, in her dressing room, Miss Hayes would look despairingly in the mirror and reflect: 'I'm nothing like Mary Stuart. How *can* I go out there and make the audience see what I feel?' When she went on stage, however, she always visualized herself as Mary Stuart, and willed the audience to view what she saw when, in imagination, she watched Mary Stuart, not Helen Hayes, strutting her brief hour.

Whether she ever succeeded in projecting to the audience the complete illusion of stature and appearance she sought is doubtful, Miss Hayes admits. But she is convinced that there could have been no illusion had she not always consciously and objectively concentrated on her own mental illusion as well as on her technique. What shocked her most in the movies was seeing herself, Helen Hayes, on the screen — 'not the character I had envisaged at all'. Every time she looks at the pictures of a play she is acting in, she receives the same kind of shock. In *Mary of Scotland* she saw: 'Helen Hayes dressed up in costume — not the slightest suggestion of what I saw, what I felt I projected across the footlights'. When she looked at the photographs of herself as the aged Queen in *Victoria Regina* she was horrified. She had built her own illusion of Victoria from a faded daguerreotype in her home. 'This woman was a totally different character — not what I looked like at all!' Only once in a photograph, in some candid camera shots taken during a performance of *Mary of Scotland*, did she receive the slightest concrete assurance that perhaps occasionally her conception did 'get across'. In these snapshots, for the first time, she discerned a glimpse of the character she envisaged. Helen Hayes was there, too — 'I suppose you couldn't expect to get rid of her altogether!' — but there was something else, 'a real feeling, both in stature and presence, of Mary Stuart'. How the camera caught it, she hasn't the faintest idea. Perhaps, at that performance, she projected the part so well that she fooled even the camera.

In acting, as in every art, there comes a point beyond which technique, intelligence, ability cannot go — when the creative quality of the actor must cast the die between mere performance and an artist's accomplishment. Any reasonably intelligent, sincere, hard-working actor can, with time and patience, perfect his make-up and technique. There are hundreds of actors available always to give competent renditions of almost any role. The quality, however, that makes the audience, not the actor, lose itself completely in the interpretation, that may, sometimes, affect even a sensitized camera film, is a purely creative one. Whatever it may be — genius, glamour, inner fire — it is a part of the endowment of every artist actor. Without it, even with a perfected technique, there can be no illusion, no projection, that is not superficial. But creative power alone, without technique to discipline and to enhance its power, to sharpen it to finer use, is likewise incapable of projecting any illusion more vital than the personality of a player. And the artist with this gift is the one who most appreciates this fact and depends least upon interpretation alone.

'The illusion of character,' Miss Hayes says, 'is perhaps the end to which technique is the means. The right conception of a role, not related technically to the theatre, is completely barren.' To illustrate: Miss Hayes, in the first days of rehearsals, is extremely backward — 'clumsy, stammering, unsure of myself, though not of my conception of the role'. Rehearsals for *The Good Fairy* were in their second week when Gilbert Miller took Miss Hayes to one side. She seemed to have entirely the wrong conception of the part, he told her. She was plain. She was awkward. There was no lightness of touch. She must — ! Miss Hayes was perfectly astounded. In her mind's eye, she saw herself in character as 'an exquisite creature, gay, fluffy, vain, irresponsible, with airy, graceful gestures'. This had been her conception ever since she read the script. She had planned the part that way. The illusion was there within her. But, owing to the slow development of technique, the idea had not, as yet, been projected, even to the other actors. 'This development is definitely a technical process — a question of counting steps, knowing when to raise the arm and so forth. In comedy, I have found that I must keep myself up, arms must be held higher, gestures must be of an upward nature. In tragedy, just the reverse.'

Miss Hayes always works out for herself in detail, before rehearsals commence, the fundamental attack on the role, the style in which it is to be played. Obviously, she and the director must see eye to eye on this problem. Otherwise rehearsals would be chaos. But once the director assembles the cast on the stage, Miss Hayes wants him to be really authoritative. The actor, she feels, should be the instrument on which the director plays. The director must integrate the performance, put the actor straight, guide him in the proper expression of the conception he has formed. Miss Hayes, to cite one instance, has 'a tendency to become monotonous in tone of voice'. She needs a director to listen to her, to advise her when to change the pitch.

While Miss Hayes likes to work with a director who is adamant, she does not respond well to one who tries to work out each bit of stage business for the actors. She prefers to develop business 'about fifty-fifty' with the director, letting him suggest the general pattern, the relation of one player to another, the ensemble, while she 'fills in the bits'. If she plays a scene badly, if she speaks a line out of key, if she fails to project the authentic emotion, she expects the director to tell her that she is wrong and try to set her right. 'That's what he's there for.' He can do so by giving her, in words, the key to the emotion, the suggestion of movement and gesture compatible with the emotion, but never by speaking the line himself or making the gesture. The moment a director starts to act out Miss Hayes' part for her, she becomes self-conscious: she is incapable of copying his actions. The gesture seems artificial. It does not spring naturally from within. She cannot speak the line, for she hears it as the director spoke it, not as she felt it.

In *Victoria Regina*, in the scene with Disraeli, Gilbert Miller — 'unfortunately' — showed Miss Hayes the gesture he wanted her to make when she offers the Order of the Garter to the Prime Minister. He held out his hand, the palm up; his hand began to tremble, he dropped it in his lap. The gesture was perfect — 'just the one Victoria would have made'. But, instantly, Miss Hayes knew she would never be able to repeat that gesture. She tried, and failed. It seemed false, 'even though it was right'. Miss Hayes believes that if Mr. Miller, instead of making the gesture, had simply said: 'You are an old lady, very tired. You are deeply stirred. You hold out your hand to confer a great honor on an old friend. Then your emotion overcomes you. You can't go on,' she would, in all probability, have thought out for herself much the same gesture Mr. Miller made. Then it would have seemed real, in character, and she could have used it. As it was, the gesture was 'lost forever'. In the scene in which Albert is shaving, to cite an opposite example, Mr. Miller, 'in a moment of inspiration', said: 'You are young, romantic. You have just been married. You have never seen a man shave before. You are interested, intrigued. Why don't you walk around and watch his face?' He didn't tell her how to walk, or where to walk. He simply suggested the emotion and its physical expression. Instantly, Miss Hayes grasped what an excellent piece of stage business could be made of the idea, and worked it out for herself. The scene was a hit every night, because Miss Hayes, spontaneously, felt that it was right — 'though, actually, it was no more correct than Mr. Miller's lost gesture'.

Playing the part, once rehearsals are concluded and the business is set, Miss Hayes always follows the pattern established by herself and the director. She does not alter postures, movements, on the inspiration of the moment, but goes through the same routine at each performance. 'Of course, you have to allow for unexpected pauses, for laughs, coughs, applause, which vary from night to night. Sometimes, too, if you feel the tempo is growing slack, it is necessary to speed it up — suddenly to speak one line completely out of tempo, much faster, startle and frighten the actors into realizing what has been happening. But, in the main, you go through the rudiments of the part in a fairly mechanical way.'

Miss Hayes is definitely and violently opposed to the theory that an actor should lose himself in the part each night, actually feel the emotion he is portraying. No actor, she thinks, can possibly let the emotion of a part run away with him and be anything but an amateur. One great performance, conceivably, might be given in a state of trance. But not more than one. Miss Hayes does not deny that emotion must play a part in the creation of a role. At some time or other, she believes an actor must feel the role. But never in an actual performance.

There is usually one rehearsal in which she goes through the part with real feeling, where she consciously allows the emotion of the role to affect her. Thereafter, she simulates what she has felt. While she is acting, she is always checking her performance in an objective light, standing off in the wings and watching to see that her conception does not falter. An actor, she believes, must have experienced in some manner, even if only in a vivid imagination, an emotion corresponding to the one he has to portray, if his conception of the part is to be right in feeling. 'But all this comes before you stand in front of an audience.' Miss Hayes, herself, has what she calls a guide to every emotion stored away — 'like the nuts a squirrel hides' — in her mind. There every impression, every emotion is filed for future use.

Sometimes the key to the emotion may spring from a completely vicarious source. Trying, for instance, to analyze the character of the girl in the movie of *A Farewell to Arms*, a character quite unlike her own, a phrase in a book of Conrad's she had read many years earlier came to her mind. Conrad was describing a girl who was not beautiful or witty, who had no striking quality of mind, but who created a tremendous impression on all the men she came in contact with. 'She had,' Conrad wrote, 'the terrible gift of intimacy.' This description at once illuminated Mr. Hemingway's character to Miss Hayes. She, herself, had never had an affair with a soldier by a moonlit tomb, while the guns thundered in the distance. But, with her understanding of the girl's 'terrible gift of intimacy', she realized how the scene should be played. She felt the 'quality of emotion that must have gripped the character'. In *Coquette*, to cite a different example, Miss Hayes had to play a scene in which she was told her lover was shot. The key to this scene she found, not in life or literature, but in a picture she once had viewed in a tabloid paper — 'a terrible picture of a woman crumpled up with grief before the dead body of her husband, killed in an accident'. Miss Hayes realized at the time that sudden grief, violently expressed in movement and gesture, is almost always awkward, ugly. So, in *Coquette*, when they brought her the news, she doubled up — 'not from grief, remember, but simulating grief'. And she believes that movement was largely responsible for the stark quality of poignancy of the scene — 'though don't quote me, please, as saying an actor must double up to express grief!'

Any experience, perception, adversity or training — through life, literature or art — which enriches the storehouse of memory, upon which the actor can draw at will, will heighten an actor's powers of expression. Although Miss Hayes did not enjoy acting for the movies, she was still glad of the experience, 'painful, disillusioning though it was'. Seeing herself on the screen enabled her to correct a few mannerisms, to point and sharpen a technique already solidly grounded in stage experience.

Miss Hayes inclines to the belief that movie technique is a hindrance rather than a benefit when the player is inexperienced, though, even here, she does not want to be didactic. The main thing is growth — 'whatever its inspiration' — a constant and a conscious replenishment and nourishment of each source of supply. For the young actor, the best and quickest way of deriving experience is: 'Roles, roles, and still more roles. Whether in dramatic school or stock. But not in a long run; that sinks an inexperienced actor.' For the actor, already tested and tried: 'More and *better* roles.'

Perhaps the pleasantest role Miss Hayes ever essayed was that of Maggie Wylie in *What Every Woman Knows*. It was entirely suited to her. It was no work. She loved the part. The hardest role, and that which was most rewarding to her as an actress, was Mary Stuart. 'Roles farthest away from the actor always are the most rewarding, because there is a challenge. That is why I far preferred the last half of *Victoria* to the first.' In the role of Mary Stuart, she knew her greatest frustration and her greatest joy. Joy, when the final curtain fell one Thursday evening in Columbus, Ohio, and she knew, positively, 'that no one could ever play the role better than Helen Hayes did that night'. Frustration on the other nights, 'their number was legion', when she failed, to a greater or less degree, to project the part in its entirety as well as she did on that one 'gala occasion'. One night's illusion of perfection, however, can make up for years of stress and strain. It is the artist's reward for a life's labor.

2. Alfred Lunt and Lynn Fontanne

AS ANYONE on Broadway — with the possible exception of Alfred Lunt and Lynn Fontanne — will tell you, The Lunts approach the problem of acting in a manner all their own. From years of working together, they have developed a technique in which each actor complements the other to an extraordinary degree. The play selected, The Lunts do not waste much time analyzing it from a literary viewpoint nor do they ponder long upon nuances of character and interpretation. They visualize a drama instantly as theatre — a stage, settings, props, costumes, musicians in the pit. When they study the script, they do so with the *aperçu* of the actor, director, designer and producer rolled into one. Only after they have already begun to act out their parts do they concentrate on subtleties of impersonation, on definitions of character.

Mr. Lunt, perhaps because of his early training in stock and vaudeville, may have a more immediately intuitive, spontaneous reaction than Miss Fontanne. Reading *The Taming of the Shrew* he may be the first to feel: 'Really, this is a *shameful* play! It has something, but we've got to build it, hoke it, play it like a three-ring circus. . . . We must have midgets, acrobats, two men to make a horse!' Miss Fontanne, reared in the more gentle school of English pantomime and acting lessons with Ellen Terry, may reason a little more sharply, more analytically — though this reaction may stem as much from temperament as from training. She may inquire: 'Will midgets be *right*? Will they be the *best* people we can use?' But, between them, they reach the same conclusion. Miss Fontanne rides from her wedding on a bouncing steed, midgets and acrobats caper all over the stage. And Shakespeare comes back from the library into an actor's theatre.

The Lunts rarely plan out a scene in advance. Their first move is to learn the lines mechanically, by rote, to get them out of the way. Then, in the privacy of their home, where they do most of their work, they improvise their scenes together and 'see what happens'. They throw themselves into these extra-curricular rehearsals with even more gusto than they exhibit in their playing. Acting the same scene over and over, they discard what is bad, keep what is good, then 'polish, polish, polish'. There is nothing objective about their method. At the same time it is not a casual, undisciplined charade. No actors could have compassed parts by Shaw, O'Neill, Maxwell Anderson, S. N. Behrman, Noel Coward, Robert E. Sherwood, Sidney Howard, Shakespeare, without an essentially serious understanding of, and respect for, their craft. They enjoy themselves enor-

mously in their improvisations. But they are always careful, to the point of exactitude, to work within the script.
And always they are guided by the reactions of an
imaginary audience, composed of stern, uncompromising
critics — most exacting among them Mr. Lunt and Miss
Fontanne — a group which has grown in stature and
severity ever since Miss Fontanne first captivated London and New York audiences as Dulcy in 1921 and Mr.
Lunt romped gaily to stardom in *Clarence* in 1919.

Stock in the Castle Square Theatre in Boston ('every
different kind of play'); an eighteen-months' tour with
Margaret Anglin in a repertory of *As You Like It*,
Medea, *Iphigenia* and other plays; then, reversing the
usual order but not the happy results, knockabout training in vaudeville, with Lily Langtry — this was Mr.
Lunt's previous apprenticeship. A first stage appearance
with Ellen Terry in a tour of *Alice Sit by the Fire*;
pantomime in London — a reputed first entrance on a
tightrope; touring in the English provinces; spasmodic
appearances in London and New York, culminating in
an engagement in 1916 with Laurette Taylor's company, had started Miss Fontanne on the road to fame.
But not until marriage in 1922 and electric lights in
Molnar's *The Guardsman* in 1924 joined their names
together and a second apprenticeship began under their
own observant tutelage, and that of the Theatre Guild,
did Lunt and Fontanne, as Broadway affectionately
knows them, begin to develop the technique which is
now second nature with them.

Appearances together in *Arms and the Man, The Goat Song, At Mrs. Beam's* . . . then a theatrical separation: Mr. Lunt the racketeering Babe Callahan in *Ned McCobb's Daughter*, the first high-pressure salesman in O'Neill's *Marco Millions*, Mosca in *Volpone*; Miss Fontanne as Eliza Doolittle in *Pygmalion*, Nina Leeds in five hours of neurosis known as *Strange Interlude*. Then reunion, not yet in Vienna, but in a Viennese setting for *Caprice*, in New York and London; the sky tops of Manhattan in *Meteor*, sword play and fustian in *Elizabeth the Queen*, high comedy and gusto in *Reunion in Vienna*, high comedy and nerves in *Design for Living*. Melodrama and more neurosis in *Point Valaine*, high jinks in *The Taming of the Shrew*, song and dance, sin and sadness, amid the threatening war-clouds of *Idiot's Delight*, the capricious gambols of mortals and immortals in *Amphitryon 38* — these and other plays, other performances, cemented a union at once mystical and practical, real and theatrical. From a dramatic instinct, sharpened, heightened, tempered and chastened by years of acting experience, emerged order and discipline.

When The Lunts enter the stage door for official rehearsals, they adapt what they have already created to the playing, to the personalities, of the rest of the cast, to new ideas they are constantly developing — even during the run of the play. Working tirelessly, they seem to infect everyone in the company with their en-

THE LUNTS
in *The Taming of the Shrew* – 1935

THE LUNTS
in *Idiot's Delight* – 1936

thusiasm for acting. Rehearsals, with them, are stimu-
lating and delightful occasions.

They find it very difficult to analyze their method of
attack. Mr. Lunt dismisses all the preliminaries with:
'Miss Fontanne and I do a lot of work at home together. But I can't just describe what it is. We've done
it so long, it's become almost instinctive.' Miss Fontanne,
almost as inarticulate, calls it: 'Something that's grown
so with the years that I wouldn't know what it was. Our
playing together, and our rehearsing, is like a note of
music that we then enlarge into a chord.' Both are extremely loath to talk about technique, personally or
impersonally. If talk they must, however, they are
adamant on one point. They must take the stage indi-
vidually. 'Mr. Lunt's opinions about technique, his
reactions to the theatre, are often quite different from
mine. Just because we work together is no reason we
should be classed as a team,' says Miss Fontanne. 'What
Miss Fontanne does on the stage,' choruses Mr. Lunt
in the adjacent dressing room, 'what she thinks about
acting, is a personal equation. I wouldn't dream of in-
truding on that side of her life. You must talk to each
of us alone.'

Bowing, accordingly, to their mutual wish, we raise
the curtain to present Mr. Lunt and Miss Fontanne as
individual actors, trusting that they will pardon the
liberty taken in introducing them into the Actor's Forum
on Acting Technique as a 'team' — a course which they

themselves, by the very nature of their technique, made almost obligatory.

LYNN FONTANNE

The first essential of acting technique, Lynn Fontanne believes, is voice control — 'knowing how to pitch and throw your voice so as to fill a theatre'. This is the one histrionic facility which she is willing to admit may be classed as technique, pure and simple — one requiring long and arduous training. All the rest are amalgams of many qualities.

Timing, for instance, so vital a factor in acting, especially in the projection of dialogue by Shaw, Behrman or Coward, is 'purely a matter of ear — something instinctive, which the actor either has or has not got'. A good *raconteur* at the dinner table or in the drawing-room 'has just as much sense of timing as the actor'. The actor's timing must be adjusted to actors and to audiences. 'You might call that technique, though even that is largely ear training.' But the moment timing becomes methodical, deliberate and overstudied — simply an exercise in technique — the actor becomes like a clock ticking. 'And precision is bad. It is far better for the actor to be a little off beat, to jangle!'

Set movements and gestures, symbolizing the tragic or the comic, are absolutely meaningless, in Miss Fontanne's judgment. The actor supplies the movement, the gesture, the carriage, out of his sense of character, his natural instinct of rhythm and mobility. For a long

time, Miss Fontanne was convinced that she never used
her hands on stage, except for obvious movements called
for by the action. Alexander Woollcott, to whom —
'rashly' — she confided this belief, laughed her out of
that fond assurance. But she is, none the less, rarely
conscious of what she is doing with her hands. Instinctively, she will raise her arm or move her body as she
speaks a line — 'just as you do in real life' — but she
never, in preparing her part, maps out a mechanical
line of movement.

Technique, likewise, cannot teach an actor how to
know, before he has finished speaking a line, that the
expected laugh, the gasp of horror, the ripple of merri-
ment, will not be forthcoming on a particular evening.
That is a telepathic quality, born with the actor — an
essential sixth sense that every fine actor must possess.
The actor, perhaps, may learn by technical device how
to carry on the next line, or piece of stage business, without a pause, so that the audience is unaware of its de-
linquency that evening. 'But that, too, is something
more than technique. . . . Call it *acting*!'

In the early days, Miss Fontanne read a play pri-
marily with an eye to her own role. Her first reaction
was: 'There's *a part* I should like to play.' As she matured as an actress, she shifted her point of attack. The
play itself engaged her first attention: consideration of
her own role became a secondary step. When she first
read *Idiot's Delight*, her own part was only blocked
in very sketchily. She signed the contract, however, be-

cause she had faith in the play. 'It is the most incredible feeling,' she says, 'to read a play on paper and suddenly to realize that, four weeks hence, you must *be* on the stage a personage as remote from yourself as Queen Elizabeth, Katherine the Shrew, Lady Castlemaine of *Old Drury*, or the vixen innkeeper in *Point Valaine*.' The instant Miss Fontanne reads a play, a visual picture of the person springs to her mind. She does not attempt, however, to probe her character until she has worked on the part as an actress — a diametrically different attack from that used by Helen Hayes. Acting out the part with Mr. Lunt, improvising details of character — walk, gesture, carriage, tone of voice — she begins, 'slowly, to get into the character of the person'. And without analytical reason — 'I try not to use my intellect at this stage at all' — a conception 'gradually, mysteriously' emerges.

'Suddenly, on the stage or in the dressing room, walking in the park or motoring to the theatre, you discover something about the character you never knew even existed. In a flash, you derive a new slant on an action, a motive. Bit by bit, you sink deeper and deeper into the person. You see that you are wrong in one scene; the woman could never use that tone of voice. No sooner is that place rectified than another gap appears. This refining process continues all during the run of the play. The impersonation is never complete, though it is truer on the last night of the run — if you are a real actor — than at any other time.'

It is impossible on the face of it, for an actor to dis-associate himself completely from his own self. 'You re-main the same size and you have the same vocal cords. But, if you are a good actor, you should not be bound by your physical presence.' Creating the part as Miss Fontanne does — working inward from without — the problem of adapting her own self to the role is 'some-thing that seems to do itself'. Playing too many one-color parts, an actor is apt to imagine that he cannot play any other type of role. After acting a string of comedy parts, Miss Fontanne began to feel that way herself. Then she realized that 'acting is a bastard art, if it is an art at all. The author creates the character. The actor's only job is to go ahead and play the part. With a well-trained voice and the proper use of make-up, an actor should be able to compass any role. And the less he reasons about complexities of impersona-tion, the better.'

Although Miss Fontanne does not rationalize move-ment when she is building a part, she follows the same general routine at each public performance. Lighting cues, if nothing else, force every actor to adhere to a more or less rigid pattern. Too many unexpected move-ments, also, tend to throw the other actors into confu-sion and destroy the play's flow of action. 'Too much movement, at any time, by the way, is bad. The eye is so much quicker than the ear that movement tends to destroy words.' None the less, she says, 'you do change the part very much during a play's run. Little things, here and there, are added or left out. If a certain scene doesn't jell — and there always is a scene that doesn't — you try to go to the bottom of what you've got and find out what is wrong. In other words, you don't fritter a part away, playing it mechanically.'

This is where the 'dangerous subject' of emotion — how much, how little emotion the actor actually feels — reenters the scene. Although, emphatically, Miss Fontanne does not 'live the part' or 'lose herself' in the role, she plays emotional scenes — such as the famous 'my three men' speech in *Strange Interlude*, or the abandoned comedy love scene in *Reunion in Vienna* — with a much surer touch if she, herself, is highly emotional while playing them. 'When my senses — or perhaps it's just my nerves — are keyed to a high pitch, I find I have a sharper ear, a much quicker response, to anything going on in the audience. I have, too, an uncanny awareness of the rightness or wrongness of my performance.' This calibre of emotion is 'probably a form of self-hypnosis'. She does not actually feel the emotion, but she hypnotizes herself into thinking that she does — always being perfectly aware of what is going on, of how she is playing the part. This hypnosis, however, cannot always be turned on and off at will, 'which is probably why my performances vary so distressingly. Sometimes, you know, they are so bad I should like to advance to the footlights and urge the audience to get their money back. At other times, well, I feel they have not paid enough.'

People have often asked Miss Fontanne: 'Why is acting in a play so tiring? You work only a few hours
eight times a week.' The usual answer to this question
is that acting is a nervous job, and physically tiring from
the strain of using tremendous breath control. Miss
Fontanne believes there is still another reason why a
big role is so exhausting. 'Being the focus of thousands
of eyes produces an hypnotic magnetism which makes
the actor physically stronger than he is himself, so that
when the eyes are withdrawn and the current is switched
off he feels like a pricked balloon.'

One of the hardest roles Miss Fontanne ever played
— 'by hardest, I mean the most wearing' — was the
Shrew. 'She is not written angrily enough to convince a
modern audience, or oneself. The role has to be played
at what seems like almost a silly pitch to make it come
across at all.' As she was physically injured in almost
every performance of the *Shrew*, the role in *Idiot's Delight* which followed it 'was like going from something
which is driving you to a nervous breakdown to lying
in a feather bed'. Consequently, while playing in *Idiot's
Delight*, she allotted the role first place as the pleasantest she ever essayed.

One of the most rewarding features of this role, too,
was the way in which the part matured. Perhaps owing
to the way in which the role was written, or played, the
character was never quite projected at the beginning.
Audiences were always a little puzzled as to what the
self-styled Russian noblewoman's background really was

— whether she was a complete fake or not. Working on the part, during the summer holiday of the show, Miss Fontanne added some cockney speeches, a few bars of a song in an early scene, to indicate that the woman had a cockney rather than a Russian background and immediately — to the intense excitement of both Miss Fontanne and the cast — the whole characterization took on a new meaning, became rounded where formerly it had been flat. 'And so it goes.'

'The bad parts are the most difficult. The best you can hope to do with a bad part is to make it human, to fill in gaps.' Once Miss Fontanne had a very bad part to play — a costume role. She did not know how to play it. 'I went to the Metropolitan and saw all the Peter Lylys. I copied one person exactly, down to the jewelry. My make-up and my appearance were so startling that the part made quite an impression. But that was only trickery. In some respects, however, the parts that do one the most good as an actor are the bad parts. If a good actor plays a lot of bad parts he can become endlessly resourceful so that when, at last, he plays a good one, something happens! And then he never wants to play another bad part!'

ALFRED LUNT

If Alfred Lunt has any *idée fixe* about the actor's place in the theatre's sun, it is this: 'The actor is not a creative, but an interpretive artist. His one and *only* job is to work *within the play*, to translate the ideas of the author. The play itself is what counts.' Mr. Lunt entertains violent opinions about the actor — star or bit player — who tries to 'hog centre stage', who puts himself on a loftier plane than his fellow-actors and the author's script — 'not that I know any such actors'. The important thing is for everyone in the show to make good.

He is convinced that the reason *Idiot's Delight* was a hit is that it was a good play, well cast. 'People don't just come to see Lunt and Fontanne. That's absurd. If a play is bad, all the stars in the world can't save it. Look at *Point Valaine*. The reason Nazimova's revival of *Ghosts* was a success was not simply because Nazimova was starred in the play, but because Nazimova, a great actress, did not sacrifice play to performance. She acted faultlessly herself, but she also stepped aside and gave their share of the play to the other actors. With the result that *Ghosts* was projected as a play rather than as a vehicle for a star actress.'

It is not surprising to discover that Mr. Lunt, holding these views, always reads a play first to see whether it is a good play, only secondly to determine whether or not it is a good play for him and Miss Fontanne — or him alone — to act in. The wide range in which Mr. Lunt's parts have fallen — youth without illusion as Prior in *Outward Bound* to maturity without scruple as Rudolph of Hapsburg, Clarence to the Emperor Maximilian, Shaw's meek Chocolate Soldier to the bestial Stefan in *Point Valaine*, Dmitri Karamazov to the

blustering Petruchio — indicates great variety and flex-
ibility of interpretation in the actor. Mr. Lunt professes
to be ignorant of the actual method by which he creates a part, differentiates one characterization from
another. Like Miss Fontanne, he believes that is something that does itself. He is sure, however, that he always attempts to make each role something new and
non-characteristic of himself. He has little respect for
the actor who simply projects his own personality,
charming or otherwise.

'I never play myself in a part — at least, I never
mean to,' he says. 'Take Harry Van in *Idiot's Delight*. I
pieced him together — accent, personality and appearance — from three people I used to know in vaudeville.
I took something from each one of them and added a
general impression based on my own experiences. Vaude-
villians, I have found, may be pretty terrible when
they're giving "their all" in a number. But most of
them, fundamentally, are pretty nice, simple fellows.
I tried to put that quality in Harry Van. Externally,
I envisaged him with a pasty-faced expression — the
look you see on men around Times Square who don't
get out enough into the air — and black, shiny hair,
slicked back around graying edges. I spent about an hour
before each performance covering my hair and face with
grease to get just the effect I wanted. Perhaps it was
foolish. I could have gone on with hardly any make-up
and got away with it. But it wouldn't have been the
same thing. Harry's accent came direct from vaudeville

acquaintances — I think accents and dialects are terribly important — from standing listening to the chatter at Times Square corners.'

Rehearsals to Mr. Lunt are even more fascinating than actual performances. He never tires of standing on a bare, ill-lighted stage, watching others perform, acting himself. His improvisations with Miss Fontanne are elixir to his actor's soul. He never relies on the director to shape his concept of a part. 'If you know your job and work for the play and not for yourself, you don't need a director to develop the part for you.' The director must work to perfect every detail in the show, to pull together all the loose strings. For that matter, so must each member of the cast. *Idiot's Delight*, for instance, was really an actor's show, directed by the actors. So was *Amphitryon*. Everyone contributed something—'which was what made it so exciting'.

How Mr. Lunt achieves his effects is a question he cannot — or will not — elucidate. Technique, he admits, is part of an actor's equipment. 'But no actor can define what his own technique is, or tell how he uses it.' He is extremely scornful of theories and rules. 'No good actor is bound by any rules. It's absurd to say there are any set formulae for acting comedy or tragedy — one set of gestures the actor pulls out of the hat when he is a clown, another when he is a tragic figure. What you do and how you do it depends entirely on the play and the part you portray. Harry Van is one type of person, the Earl of Essex another. You play serious and comic scenes differently. Of course. The timing is quite different, the whole interpretation — just as it is in life. But that depends on character more than on technique. Often you do the best you can and then something happens you hadn't expected at all. You plan one piece of business to get a laugh. It falls absolutely flat. Something you hadn't thought out at all brings down the house. You can't be sure of anything.'

Mr. Lunt's somewhat inadequate description of his playing, once rehearsals are over, is this: 'I try to relax into the part and play it as nearly the same way as I can each night. But when I say relax, I don't mean get slovenly. Every performance, whether in New York or Squedunk, is as important as the opening night.' One evening during the run of *Idiot's Delight*, the whole company slumped. The pace went wrong. The show was very ragged. 'That was a terribly serious thing. We had a big shake-up. Rehearsals. You can't let things like that happen, ever. You've got to be on your toes all the time.'

Stage business, as a rule, is set in rehearsal and the actor goes through the same routine every night. In certain types of comedy, however, business may vary considerably with each performance, especially when the play is *Design for Living* and the three leading actors know one another as well as The Lunts and Noel Coward. One night, Mr. Lunt admits, in the hilarious drinking bout he and Mr. Coward staged each night, Mr. Coward — 'by accident, or dire intention' — took Mr.

Lunt's line. Not to be outdone, Mr. Lunt promptly took Mr. Coward's next line. They played out the entire scene — 'a full half hour' — with each one speaking the other's lines. 'The scene was just as funny as ever,' Mr. Lunt declares, 'but obviously ad libbing or changing business would be outrageous in anything but a very special type of comedy, and then one in which you happened to be playing with the author. Still, in every play, you are consciously studying your part, adding new shades of meaning, building it all the time. And you know what you are doing every second you are on stage.'

Rin Tin Tin, in Mr. Lunt's opinion, was 'a great emotional actor, *simply marvelous!*' But, he points out, he could never have acted on the stage. When he barked, he barked for as long as it suited his canine pleasure. The only way he could be controlled was by cutting the film and piecing it together. 'But you can't cut on the stage. That's why an actor can never let himself be overcome by emotion. If he started to cry during a scene, there wouldn't be any play. Emotion can play a big part in acting. Sometimes a role can tear you to pieces. But it must always be controlled emotion, which is what makes it all the worse.'

Mr. Lunt refuses to place on the record the names of his favorite roles, the easiest, the hardest, or most rewarding. All his roles were hard. They all taught him something. He liked them all. In general, the comedy roles were the 'toughest' assignments. 'Anyone who says comedy isn't harder to act than tragedy doesn't know what he's talking about. Timing in comedy is so much more difficult. Waiting for the laughs. Not waiting for them when they don't come, which is even more important. And no emotional undercurrent to sustain the interest.'

The chief reason Mr. Lunt hates to expound on his technique is that, despite all his experience, he is 'never overburdened with confidence at any time'. He acts 'because it's fun — more fun than anything else I know'. He loves to dress up, just as a child does. If rehearsals are his greatest joy, long runs are never tiresome to him. He is always learning new things about the part, playing to new audiences. He is never bored in the theatre. He never has been bored. The only time languor may creep over him in the playhouse is when he finds himself trapped by a reporter who wants him to describe the technique of his performance. . . . Enough — too much — of theory! Ring up the curtain! Let the play begin!

3. Nazimova

IF *The Chosen People* is remembered at all by Broadway statisticians, it is only as the play in which Nazimova, speaking in Russian, directing and acting with an obscure St. Petersburg repertory company, made her American debut in the 'Gay Nineties'. The drama was not a theatrical 'event' in its time — as the Moscow Art Theatre's American premiere was years later. It received but scant attention in the press. It was ignored by the rank and file of theatregoers. And it was practically forgotten before many moons had crossed the Great White Way. Yet among the small audience who, by good fortune or necessity, attended the opening at the old Herald Square Theatre, there are a few people who still look back to the event as a theatrical landmark, not only because it introduced to America a great artist and a vivid personality but because it was the first production to point the way to a style of acting and direction, altogether foreign to the American stage, which has exerted a major influence on our theatre.

Gone was the cloak-and-sword school of acting, so

popular at the time; in its place was realism and re-
straint, feeling and emotion expressed in psychological
instead of physical terms. Stranger still, no star held
centre stage while the supporting company hovered dis-
creetly upper left and right, fearful of encroaching upon
the hallowed domain. Emphasis in both acting and production values was apportioned according to the demands of the play. Although a young actress named
Alla Nazimova radiated qualities of ability and presence
far superior to those of the other members of the company, no spotlight shone on her. Each member of the
cast was as important as his role; the entire company,
playing in harmony, shared the emphasis and applause.
A revolutionary innovation, to say the least!

Although a few ardent enthusiasts at once grasped
the significance of the lesson that the production of
The Chosen People had to teach the Broadway theatre
and spread the word that both the play and Mme.
Nazimova must be seen, it was hardly to be expected
that an unknown Russian troupe, presenting an unknown play in an unknown tongue, should 'panic' the
town. Broadway remained unmoved. Lack of patronage
forced the group to move to a hall on Third Street,
where a repertory of Ibsen plays was presented in Russian to the accompaniment of the music from a dance
hall on the floor above and the clatter of a bowling alley
in the rear. The small band of the faithful, their numbers gradually reinforced by others drawn by 'word of

NAZIMOVA
in *A Doll's House* – an early production

Vandamm

NAZIMOVA
in *The Cherry Orchard* – 1933

mouth' praise, crowded into the hall night after night, seemingly unperturbed by the fact that 'the pauses for dramatic effect were made hideous by foreign and irrelevant sounds', as the *Theatre Magazine* phrased it.

Although the hall was not large enough for an audience that would make the enterprise pay, the enthusiasm and applause may perhaps have helped to persuade Mme. Nazimova to accept the contract tendered by an astute Broadway producer. At any rate, she remained in this country when the company sailed for home. Six months later, having learned in that short time to speak the language, she made her English-speaking debut in *Hedda Gabler*, the same play she revived in 1936. Adding the roles of Nora in *A Doll's House* and Hilda Wangel in *The Master Builder* to a quickly acclaimed characterization, she went on tour, bringing her style of acting and her personal glamour to the rapt attention of audiences all over the country.

The visit of the Moscow Art Theatre and the Moscow Musical Studio, the influence of producers like Komisarjevsky in England and Boleslavsky in America, have taught modern audiences to accept — and to regard highly — the style of acting which we call psychological, or 'spiritual realism', a style of playing that Mme. Nazimova was perhaps the first to introduce effectively into this country. In our own twentieth century theatre we are familiar with the results, both for the individual player and for the ensemble, in the work of many of the best actors and directors. But the method, and especially the long training which produced the results, still remain foreign to our Anglo-Saxon stage.

Almost all our experienced actors have been trained in the hit-and-miss school of long runs, in a theatre whose only permanence rests on the talent and perseverance of a few of its finest actors, producers and playwrights. Almost all Russian playing, on the other hand, implies a preparation for permanence, for association with a company remaining together for many years in one theatre under one director; and for the study of many and varied parts for performance in continuous repertory.

An artist like Mme. Nazimova is obviously not the result solely of training. Emotion, intellect and heritage all had their part in her make-up. As a child she studied the violin at Odessa. Four years in dramatic school, and studying direction at the Moscow Art Theatre, followed swiftly, but not casually — four years of improvisation, rigorous training in body control, voice culture, facial mobility, to achieve an ability first to understand and then to project. The logical aftermath of this training was repertory, first with provincial companies, later in leading roles in St. Petersburg and touring the Continent. Add to that background of Russian birth and repertory the creation of a long list of Ibsen heroines, an instinctive insight into character and the special gift and presence that is hers, and you have the actress who has earned the right to be known, quite simply, as Nazimova.

Nazimova's fundamental attack, one which expresses well her basic approach to acting, is best told in her own words: 'The actor should not play a part,' she says. 'Like the Aeolian harps that used to be hung in the trees to be played only by the breeze, the actor should be an instrument *played upon* by the character he depicts. All the impulse which sets him free as a technician, or artist, should stem from the creature of the dramatist's imagining. The actor himself should be a creature of clay, of putty, capable of being molded into another form, another shape. The wind had but to ripple through the trees and the harp would play without conscious effort. The actor's assignment is more difficult. The breeze which stirs the player must sift, from the character, through the player's brain, his imagination and his body. And then, by conscious technical effort, the player must create the sound or fury, sense or sensibility, which the characterization demands.'

No automatic process can teach the actor how to fulfill his task. Much depends on the individual and his equipment, much on the part. The hardest role, always, is that which is not true — 'the silly role, in which there is nothing to probe; where suddenly the actor is called upon to be charming, beautiful, amusing, out of thin air. But every part is hard. Every part requires infinite study and patience.'

Perhaps the pleasantest role Nazimova ever played was O-Lan in the Theatre Guild's *The Good Earth*. She loved that part because it was the antithesis of any she had played before — 'something square, with no kinks, all white, clear and simple; no psychoses'. By far the most rewarding, however, have been the Ibsen roles — of which she has played all the most famous. 'If any playwright can teach an actor how to play, Ibsen has taught me,' Nazimova says. 'The reason is that he is true. There is not one line, one word, whose origin of thought you cannot trace. The same is true of Chekhov. But it is a very rare quality in a playwright.'

Nazimova creates a part 'something as follows': The first time she reads a play, she is simply an audience. She judges the drama as if it were a novel, an essay or a biography. The one essential is that it shall interest her. If she falls asleep in the second act, she reads no further. On the second reading, she concentrates on her own role. 'But I never see myself at all. An actor must never see himself in character. I study the woman. I look at her under a magnifying glass and say to myself: "Is she right? Is she logical? Is she true to herself?" ' Not until the third reading, after she has analyzed the character as an individual remote from canvas and grease-paint, does she ask herself: 'Can *I* act that woman? Can I make *myself* over into *her?*'

The farther away a character is from herself as a type, the more interesting is the role to her. She approaches the part feeling: 'I am nothing. I am nobody. I have to reconstruct my whole self into this woman I am to portray — speak with her voice, laugh with her laughter, move with her motion.' If the part were written for her, this detachment would be hard to attain. Self-analysis would always intrude into the picture. 'But if you can see the person as a living creature, quite removed from yourself, you can work objectively to adapt yourself to the part. Personally, I am no more like Hedda Tesman, Madame Ranevsky in *The Cherry Orchard*, or the brooding Christine in *Mourning Becomes Electra* than I am like the earth-bound O-Lan. But if I can project the character so completely that the audience believes I *am* that character, then I have done my job well.'

The first thing Nazimova seeks to determine about a character is 'what she is thinking, what her inner response is, her feeling, when some other character is holding the stage. Once you know what she *is*, what she *does* becomes easy to interpret. . . . You see that she could not possibly wear red, could not tie a pink bow in her hair, that she must wear gray, that she must be a blonde, that she must move in a given way, speak with a certain inflection. Sometimes, even, you may conceive a character as a blonde and play her as a blonde, though you do not wear a blonde wig. Nora in *A Doll's House* will always be a blonde to me, though I have always acted her with brown hair.'

Unlike The Lunts or Katharine Cornell, who try to

get the lines out of the way at the earliest possible
moment — before rehearsals, if they can — almost the
last thing Nazimova does is to memorize the words.
Sometimes she does not even know them at the dress
rehearsal. She is so immersed in the study, and delineation, of character that the 'sides', as such, are of secondary importance. Moreover, she feels that if a part is
written correctly, the dialogue will spring so naturally
from the characterization that it will almost learn itself.
'Once the actor knows everything there is to know about
a character's thoughts — far more, even, than the author
— he should grasp the vocabulary almost instinctively.'

In the early readings, Nazimova always reads the
play aloud to herself. At one such session she lets herself go, forgets about technique and allows the emotion
of the play to carry her where it will. Studying her reactions closely, as a critic, after the 'performance' is
concluded, she makes careful note of the passages where
the emotions flowed freely and naturally. These points
remain as touchstones. Then she analyzes the 'minutest
cause behind the emotion' which she felt instinctively
and thereafter 'tunes down the emotion — or, rather,
the actor's expression of that emotion — to the key in
which it can project across the footlights'.

Nazimova has such a clear picture of the character
in her mind by the first rehearsal that, except for the
lines, she feels she could give almost a finished performance. Stage business is 'instinctive'. The director never
shapes her conception or steers her through the me-

chanics of playing. Very few directors, she has found, know much about acting. 'Still, a good director can be of far more help to an inexperienced actor than training in stock, which, on account of rushed and inadequate rehearsal, is apt to make a player shoddy. The director, however, should tell the actor only what *not* to do. If he attempts to read lines, to show the actor the gesture he should use, he is a murderer — or he realizes, unfortunately, that he has to deal with an actor devoid of brain and imagination, and therefore must drill him as he would a parrot!

'Directing is like conducting a symphony. There are musical sentences — *leit motifs* one can trace through the play. They grow and fade. Each act, like a piece of music, is divided into sections and each section has its own inner rhythm.' When Nazimova directed *Hedda Gabler* in 1936 and *Ghosts* the year before, she divided the plays into scenes. She made notes on the margin of the script: 'Scene begins here, ends here.' This did not mean that the curtain fell but merely that a new motif was born, that one thought-sequence had built to a climax and that a different attack was needed. Nazimova has always played the Ibsen dramas on the piano, improvising music for each character, each scene, 'to find the musical, the symphonic beat of the play — a rhythm not only of sound and movement, but of pause and thought, especially thought'. When Iturbi said of *Ghosts*, 'The play, the production, is like music,' Nazimova felt that he had heard, had seen and had felt the rhythm she had conceived in terms of music. Tempo, she believes, is a delicate two-edged sword hanging over the heads of the actors. The slightest slowing-up or speeding-up at the wrong time destroys the rhythm of a scene. Variety in tempo is one of the vital elements in the direction of a play.

In one of the first interviews she ever granted in this country, Nazimova was quoted in the *Theatre Magazine* as saying: 'Sincerity and the correct use of voice are the greatest things in the art of acting. . . . If I were to advise any American actors, I would say: "Make gramophone records. One false note or inflection may ruin an entire performance." ' Although the actress had long since forgotten these words, time had not altered her opinion. Many years later she begged an actor in the company to have a record made of a long speech so that he could hear, for himself, how monotonous, how flat, his rendition was. She believes that work in the movies can be of immense help to an actor for the same reason, provided he has first been well grounded in stage technique. '*Seeing* himself, he can say: "That was bad. That was good. That is a mannerism. That expressed nothing." He can feel the rhythm of his performance, can learn to recognize the value not only of speech and action but of a pause. He can learn what not to do, which is just as important as learning what to do. Hearing himself talk, he can feel the quality of his voice, the scope of its projection, can determine its ability to express in tones the thought and feeling of words. And he can realize what good diction really means.'

Once the pattern of a role is established, Nazimova follows that pattern absolutely in performance. Often, however, it is four or five weeks after the opening before she can say to herself with confidence: 'Now I have my pattern.' Until then, she is constantly experimenting, playing a scene softer, louder, more harshly; digging into the role, dissecting it until she is sure it is right. She does not change her style of acting because of audience reactions. 'A good actor,' she asserts, 'should be able to make an audience, any audience, feel what he wants it to feel. This is his assignment.' The one thing that may cause her to alter her playing slightly on a given night is a variation in the playing of another actor. 'If one actor is a little slow, you have to come in faster. If a scene lags, you have to pick it up. But no losing yourself in the part! No being transported into other worlds by the emotion of the play!'

The time is long since past, Nazimova believes, 'when an actor can rant all over the stage and call it acting'. Inspiration plays a part, sometimes a large part, in acting. 'But one is never carried away during a performance. One watches oneself always. And the inspiration, the emotion, that the actor may feel — and often does feel — depend not so much on himself or on the character as on the interpretation, on the realization that he is projecting the desired illusion.'

'First, last and always,' Nazimova adds, 'a player must have imagination. Without imagination, he might as well be a shoe-black as an actor. Imagination kindles the feelings, steers the actor through the character into emotion, enables him to reproduce feelings he himself has never experienced.' Nazimova never attempts to relate the emotion of a scene to personal experience. 'If I thought for one second about *my* emotion while acting, I would be completely side-tracked.' Her entire concern is with the character she personifies, '*her* feelings and thoughts, *her* actions and reactions'. While Nazimova, the actress, is on stage, Nazimova, the woman, exists only as a captious critic appraising the performance from a seat on a mythical aisle.

4. Katharine Cornell

THE year was 1919. The place, London. The scene, the stalls of a playhouse during the matinee of a current hit. . . . Katharine Cornell, a young American actress who had come to London to achieve her first success as Jo in *Little Women*, was seated in the darkened auditorium watching a tense drama unfold on the stage before her. At the climax of a highly emotional scene, tears welled up in the eyes of the leading lady; they fell slowly, drop by drop, down her fair cheeks. Instantly, a woman sitting in front of Miss Cornell in the audience nudged her companion: 'Look,' she whispered admiringly, 'real tears.' Through the entire house ran the same electric consciousness. 'Real tears! The actress is so overcome by emotion that she is crying. She is *actually* crying!' The curtain, like the tears, fell slowly. It rose again. The star, still in the throes of emotion, took her bow. Her face was streaked with mascara where the tears had coursed. She wiped her eyes. A salvo of applause ran through the auditorium. No one could doubt the success of the scene.

Miss Cornell was not among those to applaud. A season of trouping, the year before, in a small part in the tear-jerker, *The Man Who Came Back*, had made her realize that tears, real or glycerine, could easily be induced into an actor's eyes. How the actress in this play made herself cry, even the fact that she did cry, did not concern Miss Cornell as she walked out of the theatre. What did affect her was this: the moment the actress dramatized her own tears, held them on show, as it were, for all observers to see, the character lost her audience. Every person in the theatre thought only of the fact that the actress, herself, was crying. At the one time, of all others, when the audience should have been hypnotized into forgetting it was in a theatre watching a play, its thoughts had been diverted from the character to the actor, from illusion to reality.

Then and there, Miss Cornell made up her mind that when she had a 'big scene' to play, she would use her authority as an actress to melt the eyes of her audience rather than her own. How much better, she thought — looking into the future, perhaps, to parts like Candida, Juliet, Joan of Arc — for the spectators to believe that a character on the stage is moved to laughter or tears and, believing it, to laugh or cry themselves, and for the actor, conscious every moment of what he is doing, always a step ahead of his part, to use his powers to create, sustain and heighten that illusion! 'Acting is only the creation of an illusion of reality,' Miss Cornell insists.

'The essential thing is to make the audience believe all the time.'

Although any form of personal exhibitionism on the part of the player at once destroys illusion, every actor is faced with the necessity of building each role within the framework of his own personal presence. His body, his voice, and his ego are the scaffolding around the edifice of character which he creates. For Katharine Cornell the problem of creating diversified characterizations was made more than usually difficult by the unusual distinction of her own presence. When a young assistant stage manager, named Guthrie McClintic, had seen her act with the Washington Square Players during her first season on the stage, he had scribbled on his program the words: 'Interesting, monotonous, worth watching' — a comment kinder than any she had heretofore received from critics and friends. Miss Cornell had been told, variously, that she was too tall; she looked awkward, gawky; her features were striking but far from beautiful; her voice musical but uninteresting; her whole presence was wrong for the theatre — too marked, perhaps; she should never consider a stage career.

Two seasons of minor roles with the Washington Square Players, an arduous year with the Jessie Bonstelle Stock Company in Buffalo (playing parts of maids, scrub ladies and the like) and the road season with the *Man Who Came Back* company, endowed Miss Cornell with the technical facility and poise to confound her former critics with a gracious and charming performance in *Little Women*. But the actress had not yet solved the problem of relating her own uncommon presence to a theatre's stage. The special radiance and grandeur that was to add lustre to many insignificant plays and enrich fine plays — qualities that must have been hers even then — still shone but fitfully in the actress' performance.

The task of 'making audiences believe' is made doubly hard for the young actor by the fact that he is compelled, through inexperience and lack of opportunity, to play many unimportant roles in mediocre plays. He has to make the audience accept not only a playwright's character but often a story essentially false. Miss Cornell's subsequent career, in this respect, was no exception to the general rule. Despite her success in London, she could not get a part in New York. After a brief tour in *The Man Outside*, she rejoined Miss Bonstelle's stock company, then in Detroit, playing the leading roles in works no better or worse than the usual stock fare. Her early critic, McClintic, happened to be a stage director for the company and he not only displayed a personal interest in Miss Cornell — they were married the following year — but he coached the actress in her roles — a new one each week. 'Don't play down your height, your peculiarities of presence,' he must have told her. 'Use them. . . . Attack each part as if it were new and vital. Learn to project character through your own personality. Use your God-given gift of glamour to make audiences believe even the silly parts. When the good parts come along, half your work will be done for you, and through them you will mature.'

The role of Sydney Fairfield in *A Bill of Divorcement*, the next year, offered Miss Cornell her first chance to enact a believable characterization on Broadway. (She was engaged for this part, against the judgment of the producer, on the insistence of the British actor in the lead who had seen her play Jo in London.) The play and the characterization were an instantaneous hit. And long after the drama had been entirely forgotten, there were people who still remembered the feeling of sympathy evoked for the young girl who remained faithful to her father, shell-shocked and mentally injured in the War. A lovely character-portrait of Mary Fitton the next year (she impersonated Juliet for one scene) in the Winthrop Ames production of *Will Shakespeare* proved that Miss Cornell was not simply a one-part or a 'modern-play' actress. Years of less fruitful appearances were to follow in melodramas like *Tiger Cats, The Green Hat, The Letter* and *Dishonored Lady* — *Candida* alone, in 1924, breaking the spell of tawdry parts, giving true scope to the actress' powers and receiving, in grateful return, a glowing impersonation. Yet such was Miss Cornell's determination to make the audience care that she made Iris March, and the other murderesses and adulteresses she depicted, seem vibrant people and she built, for the moment, some universal truth out of the unreal stories these plays told. Not entirely incidental, too, was the fact that she made enough money out of these portrayals to enable her to set herself up under her own management.

Her own best development as an actress grew — as McClintic had told her years earlier that it would — out of the good parts in good plays that she then selected for production. The changing elements of character in the roles provided by *The Barretts*, *Lucrece* (the first classic role), *Romeo and Juliet*, *Saint Joan*, *The Wingless Victory*, and *Candida*, in a matured revival, gave the actress the chance to create something more than excitement. And the presence and technique — in speech, timing and projection — used to such good effect in the trashy roles, found their ultimate expression in genuine characterization.

How Miss Cornell attacks a part — more specifically, how she adapts her own presence to contrasting characterizations — is, she says, 'very hard to describe'. Where Nazimova, with the Russian background of training, approaches a role with a complete sense of detachment — feeling that she, herself, is 'nothing, nobody'—Miss Cornell quite consciously attempts to relate a part to herself. 'Every character,' she feels, 'is both near and far from an actor's own personality. The player must understand the person, have a mental as well as an emotional sympathy with the role, to act it. Then he

Ira Hill

KATHARINE CORNELL
in *The Green Hat* — 1925

KATHARINE CORNELL
in *Romeo and Juliet* (with Edith Evans) – 1934

must present it through his own qualities of mind and physique.

'There may be actors who completely disguise themselves. But if the process is absolute, I doubt if the desired effect is produced. Every part must mirror something of the actor, himself, just as every book, every painting, every piece of music, reflects something of its creator. If an actor lost his personality, the public would lose interest in him, just as it would in a Rembrandt or Whistler painting that bore no trace of the style or personality of the artist. A good actor can play diverse roles, be a distinctly different character in each one of them, and yet retain his own personality all the time. I believe, for instance, that my Elizabeth Barrett, my Juliet and my Joan were three different people. You could not imagine Elizabeth, as I acted her, behaving as I did as Juliet or as Joan — at least, I hope you couldn't. . . . The three characters, even with contrasting make-up, all looked like Katharine Cornell. But each was — perhaps I should say, was intended to be — a person with distinct individual reality.'

Acting technique, Miss Cornell believes, can never be reduced to formula. In every art, there is 'much that is instinctive, much that is subconscious'. In acting, these qualities come into play especially in the relation of the character, and the actor, to the other characters, the other actors in a cast. 'To understand one's own character thoroughly one must see it in relation not only to itself but to the other characters in the play.' For this reason, Miss Cornell always tries to hold her impressions of a drama 'in a state of fluidity' until rehearsals commence. Reading a play for the first time, she concentrates principally on her own role, to determine whether the part is suitable for her, one to which she can — 'perhaps' — do justice. Once she has decided that she likes the part, she studies the play as a whole, examines the relation of all the roles, the reactions of one character on another, the influences and emotional disturbances of the play. Then she re-studies her own part in relation to the play and to the other roles. *The Barretts of Wimpole Street*, her first production as an actress-manager, was one of the few plays she visualized at once, not in terms of the central part but as an entity. This, she confesses, may have been because it never occurred to her then that she could portray the frail poetess. (Perhaps the Iris March influence was still too fresh.) It was only later, through the suggestion of Guthrie McClintic, that she undertook to essay the role.

Although, in reading a play, certain moments are bound to stand out in imagination as scenes played by actors, Miss Cornell spends a long time studying the character before she attempts to project herself as an actress into the role. The actual development of the part is 'a slow, cumulative process'. A few obvious details — of gesture, speech, costume and manner — communicate themselves the moment the actor picks up the script. Working out the part, in terms of a stage and of herself, Miss Cornell 'develops, refines and heightens these automatic suggestions'.

As soon as the 'sides' are delivered to her she begins to 'break' the part. She reads the lines aloud, over and over, without any expression, without giving any thought to their meaning, in order to have them tabled in the back of her mind by the time rehearsals start. She deliberately leaves them 'suspended' for the first week of rehearsals and reads her part with the other players in order that her reading should not become set and conflict or jar with other voices or personalities. Listening to the other actors, concentrating on their interpretations more than on her own, she is apt herself to read very poorly for the first few days. In the first day's rehearsal of *Saint Joan*, in fact, she gave such a stumbling, frightened reading that Maurice Evans, the Dauphin, confided to a friend that Miss Cornell could never play the part. At the end of the first week, she will try out the role without sides to help her, and this time will draw on her reservoir of memory. With the lines out of the way she can devote her whole attention to character development.

The finest hair line, in Miss Cornell's opinion, separates the good actor from the so-called 'ham'. The difference, nine times out of ten, lies in 'the power of selection, the ability to seize upon essentials and throw away the alluring temptations that clutter up a performance. Almost every imaginative person has a certain instinct for acting. But few have the power to execute, to put into practice, to make real to an audience, what they see or feel. . . . Lines, situations, character, all suggest an infinite number of things to do. The artist is the one who has the ability to select, and select accurately, the right and significant things. . . . I have seen promising actors go wrong because they could not choose. They could not resist the impulse to "do, do, do".'

Rehearsals are the period during which the actor must edit his performance. After the opening night, except for minor readjustments, it is too late. Miss Cornell as a rule works out the details of stage business by herself and then lets the director 'add and subtract'. The director, Miss Cornell feels — and by 'director' she means Guthrie McClintic, for McClintic has directed all her productions since *The Green Hat* — 'is the editor, the critic, the eye of a production. He is like a conductor who, with a fine, or poor, instrument to play upon, is able to lead his men so that he obtains the best out of them. He does not set the part or impose the conception. He draws the reins or hastens the outflow, guides the actor in the direction he is taking. When the goal is false, when the actor is getting away from the play, he sets him on the right path.'

Although Miss Cornell plays the dual role of actress and manager, she is probably less concerned with the physical routine of production than most managers. Having worked for so many years with McClintic and his associates, she is able to 'throw off' all the production details onto their shoulders, convinced, through long experience, that they will be handled with sagacity. Her faith in McClintic is so implicit that she let him, even, engage a Romeo and a Mercutio in London whom she had never seen. Her main concern, as a manager, lies in seeing that the play receives the best possible production, in engaging the best available actors for all the roles. Her chief responsibility as an actress is to give the best rendition she can of her own role in relation to the play and the other players. 'And, obviously, one acts best when one is surrounded by the best actors, for the give and take brings life not only to the play but to the players.'

All the productions under Miss Cornell's management have reflected — in the quality of presentation, the 'give and take' between the actors, the lack of emphasis upon the star — her conviction that 'the play's the thing!' The increasing excellence of the Cornell productions, however, has been due not alone to Miss Cornell's ambition and Mr. McClintic's flair for presentation but to the fact that Miss Cornell, working toward an ultimate repertory company, has gradually set up the nucleus of such a troupe — a permanent director and technical staff, and actors who have played together in many of her productions, both on Broadway and on the road. She has in that way been able to start work on each production well ahead of other Broadway 'hit or miss' producing units; to take short cuts and spend her energy on fine points instead of on routine work.

Once the performance is 'set' in rehearsals, Miss Cornell changes her acting little. The receptiveness, apathy or antagonism of an individual audience have their effect. But, in the main, she follows the one pattern, though striving, always, to improve the part. 'The actor,' she says, 'is always conscious of whether he is making his points or not. He may give a good account of himself in character and yet realize that he is not making the audience understand, or feel, all that he finds in the part. Certain scenes will always worry and vex him. Instinctively, he will feel that they have not come across as well as they should. This may be due to faulty writing, bad casting, the wrong tempo, lighting or scenery, as well as the playing. Whatever the reason, the actor always struggles with such a scene. He will try different readings, gestures and movements on different nights, but only after he has thoroughly considered, and practised, each in turn. Often it takes long playing to make a characterization satisfying to an actor. It took many months to break through the shell of Juliet. And if I played the part until I was ninety — which I shan't — I am convinced I would still find things to do, or, more likely, not to do.'

When a playgoer says to an actor, 'You *lived* the part!', he thinks he has paid the player the highest possible compliment. But the good actor, Miss Cornell declares, 'does not live the part; he cannot live the part. All the actor does is to recognize the emotion of the character and endeavor to transmit the illusion of that emotion across the footlights.' Emotion in acting, Miss Cornell believes, is a subject which should be debated only in private among players. Nevertheless, she is willing to state — 'flatly' — that she never loses herself in a role. Nor does she believe it is necessary for an actor to have experienced an emotion, or its equivalent, in real life to be able to portray it effectively on the stage. 'The truth of that is shown clearly in the other arts.' She agrees wholeheartedly with George Arliss, who once said: 'If the actor really feels an emotion, there is no sensible reason why he should continue his performance on a confined stage. He should rush into the public square and play out the scene there!'

'Spontaneous or inspired acting — meaning that something which drops from the sky at the moment when the player, Heaven help him, is on the grill in front of an audience — is equally unreliable. By a miracle it might save an actor once. But it would be unfair to tempt fate twice. Inspiration can be of real and lasting value to an actor when he is studying a role. But, even then, the actor must be careful to see that it has its roots in his work and is not a misleading flash. . . . The actor should know, at all times, what he intends to do and he should practise each bit most carefully before he puts himself in front of spectators. If the actor does live the role at all, it is only in the sense of concentrating on it, and it alone, from the moment he reads a script until the last night of a play's run.'

Audiences often wonder how an actor can play the same role, night after night, without going stale, without losing interest in the part. One reason he can is because 'each performance is a challenge. No two audiences are alike and each audience has to be convinced. Audiences, moreover, teach a player a great deal. Their reaction is the thermometer. They cannot show an actor how to act, but they can — and do — register whether the actor is ringing true.' Miss Cornell loves trouping not only because she believes that the salvation of the theatre lies in building up a theatre-minded audience outside of New York, but because the road audiences can often teach the actor more than the sophisticated New York public. 'Their reaction is less consciously analytical, more spontaneous.' The longer an actor plays a part, too, the better he is bound to be. 'I know that after over seven hundred performances of Elizabeth Barrett, I more nearly approached Mr. Besier's characterization than I did the first one hundred times, and Juliet at my last performance was nearer to Shakespeare than at any time before. The value of repertory is great, for alternating roles gives variety and freshness. But I know that I need a continuous spell at a part to get well into it, perhaps because of my training. The important thing, as William Gillette once said, is to give on the one-hundredth or the one-thousandth night the same illusion of freshness as at the premiere. . . . Oh, it's very difficult to make it all clear!'

One of the hardest roles Miss Cornell ever played

was in *Tiger Cats*, not because the role itself was un-usually difficult, but because she was expected by the leading man to play it in the same style that Edith Evans had used in London. Another very difficult role was Leslie Crosby in *The Letter* because, as an avowed murderess, she had to fight every minute against the antagonism of the audience. Joan — 'without any ques-tion' — was one of the most rewarding parts, 'for I felt that the audience got a tremendous lift out of Shaw's play and this exaltation reacted on the actors'. The most valuable training a young actor can get is — 'banally enough' — the chance to act. 'We need stock companies and touring companies. Young people must learn their craft with seasoned actors, not novices like themselves.'

'All this,' Miss Cornell says, 'is a groping and very personal viewpoint, subject to change. Opinions alter and methods grow. We all know actors who are per-fect technicians but who can never interest the pub-lic. We know people on the stage who, truly, are not expert and yet enchant hosts of admirers. . . . The final answer — if there is any final answer — rests with the gallery gods.'

5. Ina Claire

THE vaudeville comedian is the theatre's specialist. Singing or dancing, clowning in a skit or cavorting through a deft specialty act, he parades his talents before the public. Motivation, characterization — except of the broadest kind — subtle delineation, the growth and sustained creation of an impersonation are matters beyond his concern. Whatever he may do, whoever he may pretend to be, he is always himself. His material is shaped to fit his own best capacities. He wins his audience by direct personal appeal. And, winning them, he makes them act with him.

The actor in drama, it need hardly be pointed out, employs an altogether different technique and method of projection. Imagine Katharine Cornell or Helen Hayes, for instance, playing *to* an audience in the manner — if not the mode — of Beatrice Lillie or Fannie Brice, and the distinction between the styles of play becomes almost absurdly clear. The vaudevillian has his relationship directly with the audience. He projects in a straight line across the footlights. Audience and

74

comedian act together almost as one. The dramatic actor's most direct relationship, on the other hand, is with other actors. He projects a characterization to the spectators in a broken instead of a straight line. His whole approach — his whole problem — is at complete variance with that of the music-hall comedian.

The line that separates the comic revue headliner from the *actor* in comedy is, however, much less sharply drawn. The personal tie between actor and audience, so vital and so close an element of the variety theatre, still exists, to some extent, in every form of comedy. In the playhouse, as in real life, laughter connotes a response between personalities, either of a direct or of an indirect nature. The quicker the response, the heartier the laugh.

In high comedy — closer to drama in its special field than any other comic exposition — this actor-audience relationship is both less active and less acutely manifest than in low comedy. Nevertheless, high comedy demands a more immediate audience response than drama — quicker laughs and quicker tears. And the high-comedy actor, in consequence, has to be more aware of his audience than the tragedian. He does not woo the spectator with the frank and unabashed approach of the vaudeville comedian. Like the actor in straight drama, he creates character and plays to other actors. But, perhaps in the concerted attack of the whole company, acting as a unit, perhaps only in the air about them, there must be conjured up a measure of the same quality that animates the variety stage. The amount of the quality, its fibre and its consistency, will vary with the play. But the warm, intimate and friendly feeling between actor and audience which rough-and-tumble comedy evokes so markedly must be created to some degree in all comedy.

No matter how difficult it may be to clarify the rhyme or rhythm of this relationship, the truth of its existence is mirrored by the fact that almost all the best comedy actors, both in the present and in the past, have risen from the ranks of vaudeville, variety or revue. In that give-and-take school they seem to have learned how to capture an audience by, and for, themselves. Learning later how to *act* with other players, they have related that vital accomplishment to the building of character and the development of plot. No comedian seems to know exactly how the transition between one technique and the other is effected, or, for that matter, what it consists of. But there can be little quarrel with the statement that variety acting seems to be the surest foundation on which to fabricate an expert comedy technique; that the experience gained therein — if properly adjusted to the needs of the new medium — seems to be of incalculable assistance in enabling the actor to create the less tangible, but no less essential, relation between actor and audience, without which there would be no comedy, save the unintentional. This fact alone should be a sufficient excuse for opening a discourse on a gifted comedienne with a preface on low-comedy.

Ina Claire was thirteen years old when she joined the ranks of 'vaudeville entertainers', making her first professional appearance as a mimic. When she was fourteen she made her New York debut at the American Music Hall. She scored an instantaneous hit in an impersonation of Sir Harry Lauder, and was immediately signed up for engagements on the two leading vaudeville circuits. Musical comedy claimed her next, in both New York and London, the best remembered being *The Quaker Girl*. She reappeared in vaudeville at the Palace and the Winter Garden, and her mimicry and charm were then glorified by Mr. Ziegfeld in the *Follies* of 1915 and '16.

Up to this point, Miss Claire's training was typical of that of any good vaudeville comedian. She might easily have gone still further to become a specialist in that field, but the role of Polly Shannon in *Polly With a Past* lured her from the spotlight of the Music Hall into the softer glow of a drawing-room on the legitimate stage. And thereafter she devoted her activities to the new field.

Looking back to *Polly* — the first of a long line of successes, personal and public — Miss Claire says that the role itself taught her little about acting. 'It was the easiest part I ever played. The character was a girl, like myself, imitating a bad girl. I knew exactly what to do. It was hardly acting.' Opening the following year in her first starring role — Jerry Lamar in *The Gold Diggers* — she was still a vaudeville entertainer in all but name. And she might have remained one had she not, during the run of this play, discovered what acting meant.

It happened like this: The part itself was a very bad part. Miss Claire said to herself, 'This is my first starring part. It's no good. I can't do anything with it. I shall be a flop!' A friend, watching a few rehearsals, told her she was 'worse than the part'. Gradually, Miss Claire realized that she wasn't acting. She must learn not to back away, to stand still, to stand up. A gold-digger didn't shrink. She must study the character; and then she must act the part. . . . Even after the critics' warm accolades of praise on her opening night performance, she knew she was still 'bad'. Her youth and charm, her ability as a mimic, her comedian's technique had fooled the critics. But she was still not an actress.

'What can I do?' Miss Claire asked herself. 'The play is a hit. They think it will run for two years. I shall go crazy playing the part.' 'Learn to play it as it should be played. Learn how to act,' was the answer.

Miss Claire accordingly 'went to work'. Every day she studied scenes with a teacher. At each performance she tried out new bits of interpretation, new gestures, movements and intonations. By the end of the first year, she was 'a new person, an entirely different character'. By the end of the second, she was 'an actress'.

The Gold Diggers showed Ina Claire not only how to relate a comedian's technique to comedy playing but how an actor could learn to act through acting. 'Obviously,' she says in retrospect, 'the ideal training is a variety of roles. But if the actor is never satisfied, if he uses every performance as a means to an end, to learn something new about acting and about the character he portrays (no matter how silly the character may be), a two-year run can be as rewarding an experience as two years in stock or repertory.'

It was fortunate that Miss Claire learned this lesson when she did. For a happy, or unhappy, fate was to decree that almost every play she appeared in subsequently should run for two seasons. A series of brittle and amusing parts lay ahead in drawing-room comedies like *Grounds for Divorce* and *The Last of Mrs. Cheyney* — 'fireworks, tricks, technical exercises. At times I thought I'd go crazy!' Six years later, when Somerset Maugham's *Our Betters* provided a severer test of her mettle, she proved that type parts had not dulled the edge of her technique. In motion pictures, where she next gravitated, Miss Claire missed the audience frightfully. Accustomed to the instant response of laughter, the close interplay with the spectators, she found it almost impossible to project a comedy line into thin air. It was not all wasted effort, however. 'You can fake on the stage; you can't fake in front of the camera. You can watch yourself, correct mannerisms, build for points.' Her technique, if anything, was surer when she appeared for the Theatre Guild in S. N. Behrman's *Biography*. And her performance two seasons later in the same author's *End of Summer* was acclaimed as the most gratifying of her career.

Surveying the record, Miss Claire wishes that managers had not insisted on type-casting her. She would have liked to try different kinds of parts, to play some of the great dramatic roles. In one breath, she is inclined to feel: 'I got into the entertainment business early in life. Now, I'm just a compromise.' In the next (Broadway producers please copy): 'I've learned a lot from a lot of silly parts. Now I'd like to try something worth the effort.' Whatever roles lie ahead, it seems a fair assumption that each part — however good or bad — will add something to her special lustre. For Miss Claire has the same firm conviction as Katharine Cornell (which she expresses in almost identical terms) that 'the vital thing in acting is to make the audience believe everything you do all the time'. A conviction which usually seems to bring its own reward.

Acting, Miss Claire believes, if reduced to formula — 'which can't be done' — might consist of the following ingredients: talent, creative ability, experience, memory, work, capacity for emotion, to which should be added 'a lot of technique first, a little inspiration afterwards, then, perhaps — yes, surely — a dash of hypnotism. Inspirational acting has largely to do with

INA CLAIRE
in *End of Summer* – 1935

INA CLAIRE
in *Biography* – 1932

conceit. If an actor plays a part on sound technical prin-
ciples, as a musician plays a piece of music, if he has
complete control of his body, his mind, his emotions and
his will, he can make an audience react as he wishes it
to react. The trick of acting is not to make it look like
acting at all. But an actor must have a clear technique
to let his words and actions speak simply to an audience.'

By technique, Miss Claire does not simply mean a
cut-and-dried routine of movement, gesture, posture or
diction. These are only its external manifestations. 'The
actor,' she says, 'has to use a little bit of all things in
his work. He should know something of the funda-
mentals of all the arts. He should know the meaning of
words. . . . You'd be amazed how few actors do know
the meaning of the words they pronounce. . . . He
should observe carefully, all the time, the life around
him, and within him; he should make mental notes
of places, people, things and ideas. The actor can train
his body, his voice, to do almost anything he requires
of it; he can make it work almost automatically. But
to know what to make it do, how to use it correctly
in varying situations — applied technique, you might
call it — he must have a fund of knowledge to draw
upon.'

All good acting, Miss Claire says, is in a sense character acting. The actor must re-create the part, re-see
it each time he plays it, and, more important, he must
transmit this re-creation over the footlights so that

it is fresh at each performance. The moment an actor lets himself go, begins to wallow in a role, he becomes a ham.

Most non-professional audiences — 'alas!' — have a tendency to enjoy exhibitions of bad acting. The applause is often deafening after a piece of playing which the actor, 'if he is honest', instinctively knows to be ham. The actor, as a result, must be doubly on guard to control himself. For once he succumbs to the temptation of exhibitionism, he is apt to fall back on inspirational playing every time he is tired or audiences appear to be unresponsive. Miss Claire is convinced that people can be made to feel a deeper emotion, whether of laughter or of tears, if the actor forces them to realize, consciously and technically, that he is making an effort to control that emotion.

As to emotion in acting, Miss Claire holds this belief: 'The ultimate quality in the theatre, as in life, is emotion. The actor incapable of feeling emotion himself could not expect, no matter how brilliant his technique, to move an audience. At some time, but not during a performance, he must feel the emotion which is behind every event in a play, comedy or tragedy. He must determine whether the emotion is mental or muscular, whether it springs from the head or the heart, the feeling or the nerves. Then, recognizing the feeling, he can work it out technically into form, shape and substance. I believe that an actor will play a part better if he renews the emotion in his mind each time he assumes it on the stage. He should partly feel it, but his mind should direct and control his feeling. Heart and Art! It can be quite a mechanical process. But the important thing, in the end, is not how *you* feel a part, but how you make an audience feel it.'

Many years have passed since Miss Claire stood alone in the spotlight aping Sir Harry Lauder. Her technique has developed into that of an actress rather than a mimic. But she has not forgotten the value of making her points and she carries this knowledge even to her appraisal of the dramatist's script. Reading a play, Miss Claire usually skims through it quickly until the last act, reads that carefully, then goes back to try and 'build, build, build for points', to determine whether the author has created the character authentically in the first scene, whether she can logically develop the character. The actor, Miss Claire insists, should be just as aware as the author of the importance of establishing a character clearly and sharply the moment he makes his first appearance on the stage.

In the early stages, Miss Claire spends considerable time studying the play as drama, and the interrelation of all the parts. Then she analyzes her own role carefully, alone and with the author. 'What does it mean? What is it all about? What is the intention?' are questions that must be answered before any further work is done. If the character is clear, these questions as a rule present few problems. In a complex characterization, or one that is not well drawn, however, the task is not so easy. 'You even, sometimes, work up an interest in the part that the author did not intend.'

The role in *End of Summer* was one of the most difficult Miss Claire ever had to analyze. For a long time, she could not make up her mind what type of woman she was meant to portray. 'She didn't belong to the Colony Restaurant set. She wasn't like anyone I had ever seen or heard of. She was a complete parasite. I didn't know whether Mr. Behrman wanted the audience to like her, or not. As I saw her, there seemed no possible reason why anyone should like her. And yet, in that type of play, if the audience had no sympathy for the character, they would not even be amused at her. There must be something in the character I didn't grasp.'

It was not until two days before the out-of-town opening that Miss Claire finally realized how she must play the part. Sitting down with the script, determined to find an index to the woman's character, she read, 'I was brought up to care only if people were charming and attractive.'. . . 'She has a gift of innocence.'. . . 'An only child'. Suddenly the woman stood before her — 'a delightfully spoiled creature, someone who had always been protected from life, a silly woman and yet one you could feel sorry for simply because she was totally unequipped; not a complete fool, not wholly inane, even though she had "no mind", but only unprepared to cope with the experiences with which life suddenly faced her.'

With this new slant on the role, she conceived the part in an entirely new sense; she played it to get her laughs through being a pampered infant, 'completely gaga about everything'. At first, she was too obvious. The worst performance of all was on the opening night — 'I'm so tied up with nerves on all openings that I'm likely to fall back on tricks, to overplay the part.' But gradually she worked out the characterization.

'It was always a hard role to play,' she declares. 'There was only one scene — luckily the opening one — in which I had many funny lines to say. The rest of the time I simply fed lines to the other players, and any actor will tell you it's hard to get a laugh that way. . . . Once the audience realized, however, that it was expected to laugh at the character, I was able, by using a lot of tricks, to make them laugh at lines that were not funny at all.'

Studying the script, once she has mastered the character, Miss Claire scribbles rough notes in the margin to guide her — 'warm, fast, slow, pause, with feeling'. In this way, a certain 'rough pattern' for the role is established. These directions are not necessarily unalterable. She may change the form several times. But, usually, her instinctive reactions are right. During rehearsals — until the opening night — Miss Claire is 'critical, negative'. She reads the part, on stage, 'like a dumb child of six'. She is slow in learning her lines. She never, in fact, 'gets much done at active rehearsals'.

She does her serious work in the evenings at home, when she dissects the part and plans her attack. Then it is that she acquires 'a vision of the whole thing — play and part —' and works out the manner in which she can project it. In the 'old days', she used also to calculate each movement. 'Now movements, gestures, come more or less instinctively. You realize you have to play the part as it is written, if there is anything in it. You know instinctively — or you should know — whether you want to point up ugliness, beauty, humor, tenderness, what the organic qualities of the part are, the style in which it must be played. External characteristics — the walk, the carriage, the tone of voice — spring from this knowledge. You work out the whole part as something outside of yourself. When that is done, you try to blend the conception with your own self.'

Potentially, an actor should have the qualities to enable him to play any kind of role. Actually, his best role is always the one to which his temperament naturally leads him — 'not a part which is like himself, for that would be the most difficult part in the world to play, but one which comes completely within his understanding'. Miss Claire believes that the easiest part for her to play would be a simple character-role like a charwoman. 'Any ordinary actor can play extremes. The hard parts are the middle ones, when the character is neither young nor old, squalid nor fresh, when he is quiet.' An emotional role is not perplexing 'because half your work is done for you. Everyone has emotions. Everyone responds to emotions.' Wit and comedy, dependent on 'words, emphasis, timing, accents, mental things', are extremely difficult to project. The hardest parts of all are those 'that are not really sound'. Then the actor has to think: 'What can I do that the author hasn't done? How can I fill in what he has left out?'

The actor who relies on the director to shape his conception of a role and mold him into the desired shape, form and substance, is not, in Miss Claire's opinion, an actor; although youth and inexperience, of course, need guidance. Timing, tempo and rhythm are fundamental questions of talent, of ear, with the actor. 'A director has never told me *how* to play a role. If a scene, a speech, confuses me — if I don't know its meaning — I will consult him, the author, anyone who can put me straight. The director can help an actor. He can point out where he is wrong, where he may fail to produce the right illusion. Possibly, he can "beat into an actor" the proper sense of relationship of one player to another. But there are certain things every actor should know instinctively.'

Miss Claire likes to work out the details of stage business for herself. She would 'dry up' if a director tried to show her what to do. Few directors, she thinks, know very much about acting technique, even about the value of such a detail as placing an actor. 'If you are in the right spot on the stage, you can put across a line, a piece of stage business, quietly. If you're in the wrong spot, you've got to work hard, up-stream, to get the same effect.'

After 'getting through' the opening night as best she can, Miss Claire sticks 'more or less automatically' to the general pattern of a role, but she never 'expresses a scene twice in quite the same way'. She learned from Duse that 'you don't have to play a scene in identical fashion each night, provided you project the same idea. That helps to keep your performance fresh and fluid.' She will not consciously alter a part because of an audience, believing, as emphatically as Nazimova, that it is the actor's job to bend an audience to his own will. If the other actors drop a scene, she will 'pull it up, *sharp* things a bit so that they realize what has occurred'. The main things she works on are points in her own performance, 'learning new things about the part, about acting'.

'The more you know about technique', she says, 'the less you depend on the audience' — a parting thrust which serves better than any other, in its apparent contradiction, to emphasize the fact that the audience is, for Miss Claire, as for any gifted comedy actor (or vaudevillian), the main point of approach.

6. Burgess Meredith

THERE are as many theories rampant concerning methods of technical training for the young actor as there are styles of acting itself. Every school of the drama has its own doctrine; every artist or man of commerce in the theatre, his own conviction; and there is something to be said for almost every hypothesis. No oracle can speak with final assurance and say: 'This theory is omnipotent.' No opinion is incontestable. It is not through any inherent, absolute rightness in them that the conclusions reached from an actor's personal experience are illuminating, but simply as reflections of the actor's accomplishments, the quality of his artistry, the craftsmanship of the theatre in which he works.

When Burgess Meredith hazards the opinion that 'the actor's best opportunity to learn his craft lies in the chance to work under a good director', he lays no claim to originality or to infallibility. The actor who achieved stardom in *Winterset* at the age of twenty-eight and who preferred to be 'featured' the following year in *High Tor*, says, quite simply: 'I am sure that I never would have had any success if I had not been lucky enough to play under excellent direction, both in New York and in summer stock. Directors, I don't mind saying, made me. Without their aid and inspiration, I should still be sitting in casting offices. A really good director, I think, can teach the novice, in one production, more about himself, more about acting, than years of misguided playing in stock or repertory.'

So far as Meredith is concerned, these remarks are prompted by no false modesty. In his experience, the director has been 'all-important' — that much is a matter of fact. He sincerely believes he would 'flounder helplessly' without astute direction. Yet his point of view — as he himself admits — reflects his youth and limited experience. As he grows in maturity, he may not rely so implicitly on 'stern guidance'. There are implications, however, in what he says about the importance of the director which can (without straining for effect) be read into both his experience and the opinion he bases upon it — implications that seem to presage a change of focus in the theatre of the rising generation.

Few mature players who have received their training in the Anglo-Saxon theatre would stress the importance of the directors under whom they played in their youth as a major force in molding their talents. The theatre in which Helen Hayes, The Lunts, Katharine Cornell and Ina Claire served their apprenticeship was, essentially, an actors' theatre, in which plays were built around stars and star parts. Meredith's theatre seems to be headed towards a different goal — a theatre in which, to quote Meredith again, 'the director's control is absolute'. And his experience is an indication, at least, of the fact that a new approach to acting, which centres to the playing group as a unit and not to a single player, is already well over the threshold of our stage.

Meredith does not understate the case when he declares that he was fortunate in his directors. His tutelage began under the shrewd and observant eye of Eva Le Gallienne, first in her apprentice school and then in her Civic Repertory Theatre. He played no big parts there but a large variety of small roles. In the summer seasons, to vary the routine, he stormed the barn theatres as Marchbanks in various revivals of *Candida*. The first role that brought him sharply to the attention of Broadway was that of Red Barry in *Little Ol' Boy*, the Albert Bein play of reform-school life, which was staged by Joe Losey in the spring of 1933. Brooks Atkinson said then of him: 'Burgess Meredith puts into the role all the implications and shades given it by Mr. Bein' — high praise for a first major assignment.

When *Little Ol' Boy* failed, Meredith returned to Fourteenth Street and threw himself, almost at one and the same breath, into impersonations of The Duck, The Dormouse and Tweedledee in *Alice in Wonderland*. November of '33 found him again on Broadway, cavorting upstairs and down as the tap-dancing Princeton student in the riotous *She Loves Me Not*, this time under the precise, vigorous and meticulously-paced direction of Howard Lindsay. In that play, as in *Battle-ship Gertie* under Arthur Sircom's baton a year later (the play ran for only two nights), Meredith gave evidence of having a robust comic quality which responded well to direction. But he hardly led the critics to believe that he could compass a part like that of Mio in *Winterset* in less than a year's time.

To Guthrie McClintic must go the credit for drawing out of Meredith the qualities which led him to be dubbed 'the Hamlet of 1940'. McClintic, however, would be the first to insist that what he did was not to impose his stamp on Meredith but to set free in the young actor the talents for which he could not, himself, find release. McClintic directed him first in a small role in Miss Cornell's revival of *The Barretts*; then, again with Miss Cornell, in the part of the half-mad youth in *Flowers of the Forest*, when, to quote John Mason Brown, he 'came near to walking away with the production'; the next year in the savage, poetic intensity of *Winterset*, and in *High Tor* in 1937. It might not be amiss to note here, as an aside, that what Meredith calls his 'luck' has held not only with directors but with dramas. Few actors have been granted the opportunity, so early in their careers, to essay a part like that of Mio, and to learn from it truths of acting which only fine parts can teach. Perhaps that is one of the major virtues of a director's theatre — when a director has not only the vision to recognize undeveloped talent

but faith enough in his own judgment to risk a fine part
on his ability to make the actor compass it.

The director's primary job, Meredith holds, is 'to
designate a form for a part'. The form need not be a
fixed, rigorous mold in which the actor has no chance
to expand ideas of his own. Like Helen Hayes, Meredith responds much better to direction which suggests
the impulse but does not denote its expression. Staging
which aims to shape an actor's whole conception, which
illustrates each gesture and supplies each intonation,
makes him feel 'stifled, self-conscious'. He prefers to
work with a director, like McClintic, who 'lets the actor
feel his way around, ascertains where he is going and
then guides him along the path. But whether the director', Meredith continues, 'indicates the form at the beginning or the end of rehearsals, whether the form is
more, or less, stringent, is unimportant as long as he
says "yes" and "no" with definitiveness at some point
during rehearsals.' Absent-treatment direction is not
Meredith's ideal.

'Form,' as Meredith views it, 'is the theatrical relation of the actor's own conception of a part to the play
and to the other actors.' It is expressed in the stage business, the tempo of speech and performance, and, most
important of all, in the rhythm of an entire production, when the individual is subordinated to the play as a
whole. The majority of actors like to create their own
stage business. Meredith, however, prefers to have the

director suggest the business. 'I would never have the imagination,' he says, 'to think up the stage business. Unless the director told me to move, I would probably stand still' — a passive state of mind which his acting certainly does not suggest and which, he admits, may spring from lack of experience rather than an innate inability to move on his own volition. If the director makes a suggestion which Meredith feels, instinctively, is not in character, he will tell him 'after trying it out two or three times' that 'it doesn't work on this particular machine'. Then the two of them will either fight it out or compromise. 'The main thing is for the actor to be plastic — though not putty — in the director's hands.'

It is after the first complete run-through of the play that the director assumes his 'all-important' function. 'Having viewed the drama in its entirety for the first time, he tells you from the copious notes he has made: "That line was strident. That one was soft. That speech didn't mean anything; it conveyed no feeling. . . . The act lacked humor, poise or assurance. It was self-pitying, or too strong." Then it is that the director teaches the actor how to see the play as a whole; to realize where his performance is in, and out of, key with the other interpretations.'

The less creative the actor is, or thinks he is, the better, in Meredith's judgment. 'If the actor is an artist at all, he is strictly an interpretive artist. The more translucent he is, the easier it is for him to adapt himself — or to let the director adapt him — to various types of roles.' Meredith is somewhat sceptical of the 'value or the sense' of any analysis an actor may make of his own technique. 'The important thing for the actor is to achieve effects. Let the critics worry about how he succeeds or fails.' For this reason, he will only 'sketch briefly, and somewhat fearfully' a few salient characteristics of his approach to a performance.

Meredith has one 'peculiarity' which makes itself apparent at the very outset. He cannot, he has discovered, form 'a definite feeling about a play as a whole' except when it is read to him. If he reads a script to himself, he reads mechanically until he reaches his own lines and thus loses the essential impression of the drama. All the best plays he has acted in were read to him first by the author or by the director. And, in each case, he 'signed up' before he ever glanced at the manuscript himself.

Once the part is delivered to him, his immediate reaction is in the first person singular: 'What am I going to do? How am I going to deliver this line?' And, most important of all, 'What *am* I?' He reads his sides aloud 'to obtain certain instinctive reactions about the character and the playing'. His next move is to determine: 'What characteristics of this person do I know from my own feelings?' No part was ever written, he believes, which does not have in its main conception some relationship to the actor's own personality. The character may be weak, strong, arrogant, supercilious, snobbish, headstrong. The actor, himself, may not be any one of these things in whole, or even in part. But, certainly, he will have had moments in his life when he experienced the emotions these qualities produce. 'He may not have killed anyone, but there are times when he would have liked to!'

Meredith next tries to recall the reaction the emotion produced in him at the time he felt it. With that as a base, he then 'dresses the character' in his mind, and endeavors to make it conform to his ideas. If the character is a conceited prig, automatically he reads the part, feels the part, as if he were a conceited prig. If the person is shy and defensive, he approaches the characterization shyly, defensively. 'From that point of view technique is simple. The only thing that really counts is: Does it get across? Does it project?'

The moment rehearsals start, the whole conception of how to read and play a part — 'not the conception of the part itself' — is apt to change. In the privacy of his home, the actor may strike 'some perfectly grand inflection for a big line'. The instant another actor gives him the cue, however, he is apt to realize that 'the inflection is all wrong'; the tone of voice of the other actor, his tempo or movement, has killed it. The reading is out of key with the style of the play. The same type of realization is apt to occur after the first audience reaction. Then the conception may have to be altered 'to fit what goes over and what doesn't'. It is

BURGESS MEREDITH
in *Three-Penny Opera* – 1933

BURGESS MEREDITH
in *Winterset* – 1935

extremely difficult to be sure, especially in comedy, that a line or scene will affect the audience according to advance expectations. '*Battleship Gertie,* for instance, was so funny in rehearsals that the technicians watching the dress rehearsal were literally rolling in the aisles. It needed an audience to prove how terrible it really was.'

Learning lines is a 'turmoil and headsweat' to Meredith. He cannot memorize a part, as most actors do, simply by reading it over and over. He must see the lines photographically. Reading the part, he conceives the lines in terms of the emotions behind them, gets 'the general idea of hate, bitterness, love or humor'. Then he writes them out — 'filling hundreds of pages of scrap paper' — until they are indelibly printed on his brain. Once they are learned — 'usually quite late in rehearsals' — they are put aside and he concentrates thereafter on the fine points of the characterization — a concentration which does not cease when the opening-night trial is over and the play settles down to a run. 'That is only the beginning. You work on the part each night you play it. You try, always, to think of it as something alive and fresh. You refine the interpretation each time you play it.' Meredith purposely alters the pattern of a role slightly each time he goes on the stage, 'in order to avoid getting into a rut'. The main outlines remain the same, but he will 'graduate an emotion, vary the shades of intensity. And, suddenly, one night, you will hear yourself giving a line twice the meaning. *That's* a great thrill.'

Every moment that he is on the stage, the actor must be able to 'hear himself'; in other words, he must be conscious of what he is doing. Of itself, this fact makes it impossible for an actor to lose himself in a role. Such emotion as Meredith may feel during a performance is 'probably a form of non-alcoholic intoxication. You tap your reservoir of emotions while you are creating the part. Playing it, you merely carry this feeling objectively in the back of your mind. You are conscious of the effect this emotion should produce, but you don't let it affect you. For instance, in a scene in which I have to be very angry, I carry in the back of my mind the sense of "I'd like to sock you in the eye!" which would probably be my own personal reaction. The words I pronounce may be altogether different, but I dive under them with a sock-you-in-the-eye feeling to find the right reaction. I don't attempt to feel angry, or even to think of what it feels like to be angry. I couldn't possibly recreate a conscious emotion each night. I knew an actor who told me that always, when he played one scene in which he had to commit suicide, he tried to think of his emotions just before he stepped into a cold shower; that was his key to the scene. When he was able to visualize the emotion he played the scene beautifully. The trouble was that nine times out of ten he couldn't get near the cold water in his mind and then was unable to project anything. If I have to play a suicide scene, I always strive to keep a physical picture in my mind, to imagine how it will feel when the bullet enters my head — the shock of steel tearing through my brain. In *Winterset*, when I was shot, I always thought of something striking me forcibly in the pit of the stomach; then I doubled up in pain. I have never been shot, but I have been hurt at sports and, knowing the feeling, I tried to simulate the effect it had on me at the time. But I didn't feel the emotion it produced.'

Like every actor, Meredith finds it 'difficult, if not impossible', to illustrate the part emotion plays in acting. The attempt to dissect his method of playing — 'if there is any method' — rather frightens him also. He is, like most actors, quite unsure of ways and means. The one thing he is completely certain of is this: 'The role of Mio in *Winterset* was the hardest, the pleasantest and the most rewarding role any young actor is apt to encounter. Difficult, because the diction was so exacting and I had, besides, to overcome the immense technical hazards of presenting a great and poetic line spoken by a lowly person.' He had to find the emotion of the lowly person and 'let it speak with the tongues of angels, without sounding silly or losing the sense of character'. Pleasant, because the role gave 'lasting pleasure. The play lifted people up. It exalted them. You felt that all the time you were on the stage.' Rewarding, because each performance was a challenge. 'Sometimes, you felt you had really realized the part.'

7. Fred Astaire

TO DESCRIBE Fred Astaire as an 'Actor and Dancer' — in the manner of that reliable and informative volume, *Who's Who in the Theatre* — is to state a simple and obvious truth. But the delineation, though accurate, is inadequate. Like the monograph on Astaire, prepared by the movie press department, which reads: 'Fred Astaire was born in Omaha, Neb. Height: five feet, nine inches. Slender. Dark brown eyes and hair. Once owned racing stable in England. Likes tennis, golf and prize-fights. Birthday, Nov. 26,' it errs on the side of understatement and tells only part of the truth. If histrionic talent and the ability to dance with grace and precision were Astaire's only attributes, he would never have been able to create a form of entertainment as popular with tennis, golf, fight and racing fans as with students of drama, dance and film — a blend of song and dance, sense and nonsense, beauty and agility with an almost universal appeal.

Leaving out of consideration the intangible elements of personality, presence or genius — which, in the final

analysis, determine the true validity of any artistic accomplishment — a large measure of Astaire's success
as an actor-dancer must be ascribed to the fact that he
is an expert choreographer, who designs, and has, since
childhood, designed his own routines. Out of an innate
sense of form, of balance and of rhythm, complemented
by a natural gift of showmanship, Astaire has created a
diversified group of dance patterns, on stage and screen,
which are almost perfectly adapted to his own special
capabilities as a dancer. Another achievement to which
the actor-dancer must plead guilty is that of being
what might be called a 'choreographer in terms of
camera angles'. As the critics have noted, Astaire seems
to be the one actor-dancer who is equally good on
screen and stage. Credit for this has been imputed
(naturally and rightly) to his excellence as a dancer
and a comedian. But little or no stress has been laid
on the equally important fact that Astaire himself (perhaps without realizing it) has evolved a method of
photographing the dance which sets free its qualities as
a medium where formerly they had been stifled. To
add another item to the tally of attributes, it should be
noted that Astaire, without any voice, in the operatic
sense, has found a way to inject a dancing rhythm into
song which makes his singing, if not a joy forever, at
least a most immediate pleasure — as gay and buoyant
as the tapping of feet. And, as a postscript, it might
be observed that he has even popularized the dance in

the most talkative but least articulate of all mediums —
the radio.

Being imbued with a passionate dislike of anything
which is even faintly spurious or 'arty', Astaire will
probably resent being characterized as a choreographer
or as a designer of the dance in relation to the camera
angle: for one reason, because of the slightly highbrow
ring of the word 'choreographer'; for another, because
he does not like to believe that he applies that kind of
technical approach to his work. He will admit freely
that he plans all his own dance routines, thinks them
through first in the mind, sometimes even charts them
on paper or on the blackboard, and then works them out
with his 'own two feet'. He will acknowledge that he has
definite theories about the way a dance should be 'shot'
in the movies and that he plans all his own camera
angles. But try to make him concede that in this 'planning' there is any deliberate application of a studied
technique and he will shy away from the suggestion.
Like all those who really know the most about technique because they know how to apply it, Astaire is
inclined to scorn the thought that technique is anything more than 'a sort of instinctive knowledge de-
rived from years of experience'. He dislikes shackling
his technique with words as much as he objects to talking about himself — qualities which make him both
the bane of the RKO publicity department and an
extremely agreeable subject for an interview. For when
you examine his rather hesitant replies to inquiries about

his work, you discover that it is not difficult to read into his remarks certain conclusions about how the singing actor-dancer, who is his own choreographer, and a resourceful technician, applies the very technique he would like to disavow.

One reason why an artist finds it difficult to analyze his technique is that, by the time he has reached the point in his career where anyone is interested in the analysis, the technique is already second nature. It has saturated his being for so long that its application is a mystery to him. A brief résumé of Astaire's career should illustrate, better than any argument, the fundamental reason why his technique is to him (as to The Lunts) a practically subconscious asset.

Astaire started dancing in public performance at the age of five and he has been dancing ever since. At his birth, the proverbial gold spoon was strongly in evidence, not in worldly assets, but in the presence in the household of his sister, Adele, who was to become a perfect foil for him, both as comedian and dancer, in a twenty-five-year partnership. The two youngsters danced whenever and wherever they could, and a professional New York debut in vaudeville was the reward, when Fred Astaire was only twelve. There they ran into the child-labor laws and were forced to bow out of the act. For four more years (discouraging years to the dancers who were already professionals in all but name), they had to seek engagements elsewhere. But, in 1916, they were judged sufficiently mature to tour the United States and Canada, again in vaudeville, and the next year — Astaire was then seventeen — they appeared as full-fledged professionals in New York, to be acclaimed as the most talented youngsters who had graced the vaudeville stage. The following season, they danced their way into the hearts of the audience in that patriotic medley, *Over the Top*, and then for two seasons whirled through the mazes of *The Passing Show* (runway and all) at the Winter Garden. There followed a long succession of musical comedies and revues — in New York, on the road, in London and the English provinces: *Apple Blossoms*, *For Goodness' Sake*, *The Bunch and Judy*, *Lady Be Good*, *Funny Face*, *The Band Wagon*.

Then the brother and sister act was dissolved (by marriage), and Astaire had to look for a new partner. Although the ardent admirers of the Astaires believed that he could never find an associate who suited and graced his style of dancing as well as Adele Astaire — especially in the delightful, rough-and-tumble 'run-arounds' they used to do in almost every show — Astaire found in Claire Luce a partner who, under his astute guidance, danced gracefully and pleasingly through *Gay Divorce* for a season in New York and another in London. Then came the 'Hollywood offer', and the opportunity to try out his talents in a new medium, and with a new partner, Ginger Rogers.

Astaire, according to his own estimate, was 'probably the most surprised person in the world' to find that he 'clicked' as a dancer in the movies. It never occurred to him that any dancing he might do on the silver screen would be more than incidental to a picture. It was strictly as an actor, or comedian, that he hoped to romp through the golden gates of movieland, retaining enough compensation on the way out to guarantee more security than the stage could afford when he became too old to dance eight times a week. Most of the dancing he had seen in motion pictures had not seemed to have any great authority as art or entertainment. Perhaps the flat surface of the screen robbed the dance of any three-dimensional quality. Perhaps the lack of personal contact with an audience destroyed an emotional vigor essential in dancing. It was with some reluctance that he essayed his first dance in the new medium (a small bit with Joan Crawford in *Dancing Lady*) and it was not until he saw the previews of the 'Carioca' (his first big dance number with Ginger Rogers in *Flying Down to Rio*) that he was willing to admit to himself that dancing might project as well on the screen as on the stage. Oddly enough, he reached this decision not because he liked the 'Carioca' as a dance. He did not like it; but the fact that it undoubtedly 'went over', that the audience enjoyed a routine which was, in his opinion, only fair, stimulated him to say to himself, 'If they think that's good, surely I can do something better than that.' Dancing could, after all, be made to project as effectively in black and white shadows as in the flesh.

The three years of dancing on the screen that produced *Gay Divorcée, Roberta, Top Hat, Follow the
Fleet, Swing Time* and *Shall We Dance* forced Astaire
to the somewhat reluctant conclusion that his dances
were even more persuasive on the screen than on the
stage. 'From my own observation, I know that some
of the same steps that people never even noticed on the
stage are successful on the screen, and any number of
people tell me that they get twice as much kick out of
my dancing in the movies as they ever did in the
theatre.'

Astaire, at one moment, professes ignorance of the
cause of this phenomenon. In the next, he tries to find
an explanation for it — and out of his explanation
emerges (perhaps unwittingly) the clue to his success
in the motion picture medium — the very simple
method, in short, which he evolved to make the dance
register photographically.

'In the old days,' he says, 'they used to cut up all
the dances on the screen. In the middle of a sequence,
they would show you a close-up of the actor's face, or of
his feet, insert trick angles taken from the floor, the
ceiling, through lattice work or a maze of fancy
shadows. The result was that the dance had no continuity. The audience was far more conscious of the
camera than the dance. And no matter how effective
the trick angles and cock-eyed shots might have been
in themselves, they destroyed the flow of the dance

— a factor which is just as important on the screen as on the stage.

'I have always tried to run a dance straight in the movies, keeping the full figure of the dancer, or dancers, in view and retaining the flow of the movement intact. In every kind of dancing, even tap, the movement of the upper part of the body is as important as that of the legs. Keeping the whole body always in action before the camera, there are certain obvious advantages that the screen has over the stage. You can concentrate your action on the dancer; the audience can follow intricate steps that were all but lost behind the footlights, and each person in the audience sees the dance from the same perspective. In consequence, I think that the audience can get a bigger reaction watching a dance on the screen than behind a fixed proscenium arch — probably because they get a larger, clearer and better-focused view, and so derive a larger emotional response.'

Chorus numbers, Astaire believes, should be used sparingly. Shots which show a thousand girls pirouetting, or in military formation, are meaningless because there is no individual audience reaction to that type of dance. 'Chorus numbers should be used only when you have a definite idea of something for the chorus to do which will heighten the whole dance number. On the stage, you can bring them close to the audience and get a visible emotional reaction. In the movies, the chorus should be used largely as background, because you cannot recreate that same kind of reaction. By the time you line up thirty girls in the forefront of a screen, they are so small that their individuality is lost.' Astaire disagrees fundamentally with the theory that every big musical film must contain one 'flashy number with lots of girls'.

In planning out the angles from which to 'shoot' the dance, Astaire is always guided by the principle that the audience should never be aware of the camera. He places it at approximately eye-level and lets it shoot the dance as 'straight on' as possible. Usually, he shoots a sequence with three cameras, working simultaneously. The 'A' camera is allotted the position he thinks will be best, the 'B' and 'C' cameras are placed at either side of it. Each 'take' is thus recorded, in entirety, on three rolls of film. When the 'rushes' are viewed the best shot is selected for use in the finished film.

'The "B" rush, taken a little from one side,' says Astaire, 'sometimes has a more interesting composition than the direct shot. One shot may be more alive than the next. It is almost impossible to be sure which re- cording will be the most satisfactory; the eye of the camera is so different from the human eye. It can look at you from different angles, follow you without alter- ing the perspective. If possible, one "take" will be used for the whole dance. If, however, the "B" take is much better in one sequence while the "A" is better in an- other, the best sequences are pieced together, but the sequence of the dance itself is never broken. The audience may be conscious of a change of angle, but it will never be conscious that the flow of the dance has been interrupted.'

Astaire plans his dances for the screen in the same manner he used for the stage. 'On the stage you are bound by the limits of a 40-foot proscenium arch, whereas in the pictures you have a little more scope, though not much more, as the dance should not wander all over the lot. What the first approach is, is almost impossible to tell. Often the story, the character or a piece of music will be the inspiration for a dance routine. Sometimes the conception will come right out of the blue. You get an idea that it would be swell to do a dance on roller skates, or to your own shadow. When this happens, you have to fit your idea into the book, or, perhaps, even build the book around the idea. For instance, I had the idea for the *Top Hat* dance long before the picture was planned. The picture, even its title, grew out of that idea.' Generally speaking, however, the book is planned first, and the dances are then built around or fitted into the framework.

This 'fitting' process may vary with each dance, but usually the next step — 'an all-important one' — is to have the music written. 'I find that I have to have music that will give my idea some inspiration before I start working out the actual steps. If the music is bad, I am completely stumped. I can't do anything.' Once the music is written, Astaire begins to devise the pattern of the dance. He experiments a great deal with the steps, always remembering that each dance has to be something new, as well as something good.

'Working out the actual steps,' Astaire says, 'is a very complicated process — something like writing music. You must think of some step that flows into the next one, and the whole dance must have an integrated pattern. If the dance is right, there shouldn't be a single superfluous movement. It should build to a climax and stop!' As already noted, Astaire works out his own steps and those of his partner. In pictures, he usually leaves the chorus routines to the supervision of the dance director, unless the dancing of the chorus has an important bearing on his own work, in which case he will outline routines for the girls and tell the dance director what he wants. Also, the floor space available for the dance is such a vital part of the routine that Astaire tells the director ahead of time exactly how much space he will need for each dance.

Astaire will often work for weeks on a routine to get it perfected before he tries it out in rehearsal. He will rehearse it as long as necessary — the length of time depends on the dance — and, once he starts to shoot, he will keep on shooting until it is right. The average dance is recorded on film from six to ten times, each time in its entirety. But if there is something very difficult, physically or technically, about the routine, they may shoot the sequence as many as twenty times before a 'take' is selected. The roller-skating sequence in *Shall We Dance*, for example, was shot almost thirty times.

'Planning the pattern is not all there is to a number by any means. Once it is planned in the rough, you have to know how to start and end it. This may appear to be a simple affair. Go into your sequence when the orchestra strikes up and stop when it finishes. But it is not as easy as that. It is extremely important for a dance cue to flow naturally in and out of the story. I think the audience always slumps — even more in the movies than on the stage — when it hears an obvious dance cue, and both the picture and the dance seem to lose some of their continuity. Each dance ought to spring somehow out of character or situation, otherwise it is simply a vaudeville act. Also, you have to be able to sense the moment when the audience reaches its peak of exhilaration and feels like applauding. Then it's over.'

Astaire does not believe that any straight dance routine should run for more than three minutes. 'I doubt if it could hold an audience longer than that.' How to decide, without an audience, when you have reached the 'natural ending' is unquestionably difficult. It is a matter of 'training, talent, ear — whatever you want to call it'.

Astaire tries, as far as possible, to record the sound on the set, while the dance, or song, is being 'shot'. This might appear to be the only logical procedure, but it is different from that employed by most singers, or dancers. Usually the song is recorded first in the recording room, and is then played back on the set on a gramophone record, the singers matching the movement of their lips to the already-recorded song. With Astaire, the orchestration is recorded first (to avoid the expense of engaging a high-priced orchestra to wait for hours on the lot), and the singing or dance is done to a play-back, which later, on a separate sound track, is made a part of the film. The sound of the dancing — if there is any sound — is usually recorded on the set, too. But, occasionally, especially for an intricate tap, he will do the dance on the set without any sound recording and then dub in the steps in another room with a good floor, matching the sound exactly to the picture.

If you ask Astaire whether he prefers the movies to the theatre, whether he plans ever to return to the legitimate stage, he will parry your questions by saying that he likes working in pictures for several reasons: 'Even though it is hard work and the hours are very long, it is, in some respects, less of a grind than the the-atre. You have your evenings free. The holidays are longer. And the salaries, unquestionably, are much higher than anything the stage could afford.'

If it seems a fairly safe assumption that he will not return to the theatre, it is equally safe to say that he would not continue to dance for the motion pictures — no matter how great the largess was — if he did not feel that he was doing good work in that medium. For you have only to watch Astaire at work to realize how great his artistic integrity is. He refuses to do bad work, of any kind, before the public. He is never satisfied that he has done his best before the cameras. Always he is

convinced that 'just one more shot' would be better
than the last one. He is a prodigious worker and he cannot tolerate sloppiness. A scene — straight or dance —
can never be just good enough. It must be exactly right.
In one of his many radio broadcasts, he slipped up in a
tap-dance routine. He 'covered' the slip instantly, so that
no one who either saw or heard the program realized
the error. But he was miserable for days and could talk
of nothing else at the studio. So many young dancers
all over the country, he said, were listening. It was
awful to disappoint them with a shoddy performance.

Emphatically, he does not subscribe to the belief —
held by some theatre people — that it is unnecessary to
act to be successful in the movies. 'You might get by in
one picture on personality plus, but not more than one.'
The technique of movie acting is different from stage
technique. The camera can detect the ham and mag-
nify it much more quickly than the naked eye. Most
stage actors find that they have to 'tone down' their
performances in front of the camera as it tends to ex-
aggerate expression and gesture. Astaire, however, has
always been inclined to work 'somewhat on the under-
playing side'. As a result he did not have to alter his
technique very much.

'It's a different kind of acting. You don't have to sustain a scene or carry a performance for two hours, as
you do in the theatre, no matter how you feel, but it's
very difficult to shoot out of sequence and to match the
long and close-up shots. It may be a more mechanical

technique, but you have to act. Don't fool yourself about that.'

The audience, in the theatre, had been so 'absolutely vital' to Astaire — rehearsals when he played to 'thin air' were a nightmare to him — that he expected to miss it tremendously in the studios. Much to his surprise, he found that the lack of an audience 'didn't mean anything' to him. 'In the theatre, when you expect a laugh, or applause, and it fails to materialize, it is very upsetting. In the studios, when you don't expect it, you don't miss it. You don't need an audience to show you how to time your speeches' (not after years of stage training, perhaps). 'And on the comedy lines, we get the laughs in rehearsals — from the director, technicians and others—which helps us to see what will go and what won't. When we play the scene, we never consciously wait for laughs, as you have to on the stage. If you wait for a laugh and it doesn't come when the picture is shown, it is awful. Whereas if the laughs do overlap and you lose some of the lines in consequence, that is a good thing. The same general thing is true about the dances. I would much rather have the audience feel that they had missed something than that they had had too much. And it's good box-office. They will come back again to see what they may have missed.'

Astaire feels that movie technique, so called, is a help, rather than a hindrance, to a dancer's future stage career. 'A good actor can cover a line he has missed on the stage. The dancer can cover a slip in the routine. But in the movies, the relentless eye of the camera catches

FRED AND ADELE ASTAIRE
in *The Band Wagon* — 1931

FRED ASTAIRE
in the film, *Roberta* – 1934

any slip-up. On the other hand, you can take a scene over and over again in the movies until you have the supposedly perfect shot, so perhaps the two things balance.'

Stock questions — like: What is your favorite dance? What type of dancing do you prefer? What is the future of the dance? — put Astaire on the defensive. 'I have no favorite dance routines,' he says. 'I find that I usually like my most recent numbers the best.' He has a great attachment for many of the dances he did with Adele Astaire on the stage — especially the 'Run Around', and the 'Whoops' number in *The Band Wagon* — but, generally speaking, 'there is no one type of dancing that projects better than another, on stage or screen. It all depends on the dance and the dancer. Not every dancer's type lends itself to the screen. I am not sure what type does click, but I know that certain types don't — no matter how excellent they may be.'

On one general topic alone will Astaire expand with any degree of fluency: the most valuable training for a young dancer. 'The novice in dancing,' he feels, 'should get the fundamental points first — he must know what to do with his hands, which are just as important as feet in dancing. Ballet training is very useful but should not be allowed to penetrate the style, unless the dancer plans to restrict himself solely to ballet. The dancer should use what ballet can give for its value as a smoother-out process, but it should not dominate his work. First and foremost, any young dancer should realize that it is as an individual that he will make his success. You cannot teach dancing, as you can teach singing or music. You can teach only the abc's; the dancer himself must do the rest. If he does not, no matter how technically proficient he may be, he will have no character as a dancer. If the greatest dancer in the world has no stage personality, I defy him to get across! For the movies, a dancer should be able to act as well as dance. Otherwise, his field is strictly limited. And, even on the stage, the dancer who cannot act has little opportunity except in specialty numbers — which narrows his opportunities.'

From the thousands of fan-mail letters Astaire receives, those that worry him most are those asking for advice, couched, often, in the general phraseology: 'You got all the breaks. Now tell me how to do it.' He would willingly disclose the secrets of success if he could. He would like, above everything else, to be able to give good advice to young dancers. 'But what can I tell them? My own training was this: I went through ballet school when I was a very little kid — then I taught myself the rest, by doing exercises and by dancing and acting anywhere and any time I could get a chance. It was only by going through dismal disappointments for twenty-odd years, by working in vaudeville, night clubs, anywhere I could, and by learning to dance, that I got ahead. I don't know *how* you do it. But I do know that unless the young dancer is willing to take an awful lot of set-backs, he's never going to get any recognition.'

THE SINGING ACTOR

by Lotte Lehmann

THE SINGING ACTOR

BY

Lotte Lehmann

THE approach to a new part in opera is a highly individual problem for each singer. The obvious approach is, of course, through the music, and most singers focus their attention first upon the music as the only real clue to the dramatic action.

This is in direct contrast to the method of approaching a song, however. In studying a song I never begin with the music, but first consider the text, to which the accompaniment is, in the beginning, of secondary importance. I build up my songs from their actual foundations — the words — my interpretations flowing always from a deep sense of the poetry in the music. It is this poetry which inspires the composer to build up the wondrous interweaving of speech and melody that is a song; it is this poetry which inspires him to interpret the verse in his music and to create a harmonious entity. To many singers the poetry will necessarily seem secondary until it is recreated through union with the music, and thus expressed more clearly and more mean-

ingfully to all the senses. But to me the actual sound of
the words is all-important; I feel always that the words
complete the music and must never be swallowed up in
it. The music is the shining path over which the poet
travels to bring his song to the world.

For an operatic part, on the other hand, I always start
with the score as a foundation for the interpretation.
Only from a study of the score can there come a true
emotional understanding of the dramatic action of the
opera, and it is only after I am thoroughly familiar
with the music that I immerse myself in the libretto, to
study my role from its purely dramatic aspect in order
to judge whether I am suited to it.

The singing actress must always find the clue to a
character in opera for herself. A stage director can help
her, to be sure, but the greatest stage director, the one
whom one follows as a final authority, is the music. The
singer who approaches his part, looking on the music as
of secondary importance, as though he were approaching a play instead of a music-drama, is not only a bad
musician but a bad operatic artist. In the true artist there
is an inherent inner capacity to sense musical and dramatic values simultaneously, and without this sixth sense
the opera singer will never be able to give a convincing
portrayal, no matter how much study is put into a role.

The singer who is creating an operatic part is naturally less free than the dramatic actor. He is, to some
extent, the slave of the music, and must follow it and

adapt all his actions to it. I have sometimes envied the
freedom of the stage actor, who has the opportunity of
unrestrained surrender to the character he is portraying.
But when I once confessed this to a great actress whom
I admired, she answered: 'Good Gracious! — and I envy
you, who have the mighty stream of music to carry you
on, to release the underlying emotion, so that an inap-
propriate gesture or a falsity of mood is almost impossible.' On closer thought I realized how true this was.
To the opera singer the music is the basis of all stage
behavior, a fine restraining force, at the same time as it
is the root of all character interpretation.

My own acting always stems from personal experience and a mental conception of what is true and beautiful in life. But when I am on the stage I forget self
and audience, everything but the role I am playing and
the music I am singing. For only when heart and mind
fuse into perfect union can one produce a characterization of poetic vitality and basic truth.

The most rewarding parts I have played in opera
have been those in which I could express a really vital,
human quality, while still retaining a correct singing
style. A pure singing role, however, whose ultimate
success lies only in a correct vocal and technical approach and not in the living character, has never interested me. The parts I have enjoyed the most have been
the Marschallin in *Rosenkavalier*, Leonora in *Fidelio*,
Elisabeth in *Tannhäuser* and Sieglinde in *Die Walküre*,

roles of varied type; I should be sorry indeed to be limited to Wagnerian parts.

The Wagnerian singer must, of course, suit her mood and action to the nobility and flow of the music, which dictates this action. In a Strauss role, however, the singing actress must act her part freely and with seeming inattention to the restrictions of the music. That is, perhaps, why Christine in Strauss' *Intermezzo* was, for me, the most difficult role to prepare and sing. I did the premiere in Dresden, where Strauss himself was present at all the rehearsals and made very clear to me the manner in which he wanted the role to be treated. He wanted a new vocal style, half speaking and half singing, and emphasized that, although he had written exact notes for the part, he wished me rather to build up my own interpretation than to adhere too meticulously to these notes. As Christine I played the part of a shrew; in her scolding and tempestuous moods I was required to be fully cognizant of the music and yet to subordinate it entirely to the action and speech. I found it very difficult to acquire this technique, but Strauss was pleased with the results. Probably the reason this role has never become popular in Europe is because its new singing style is completely foreign to the usual opera technique.

To sing the Marschallin in *Rosenkavalier* on one night, striving for a mellow, understanding characterization, and on the next night to sing the youthful, passionate Leonora in *Fidelio* is to exercise one's full range of emotions. It is continual exercise of this sort from which the singing actress and her audience benefit, the actress acquiring new means of expressing music and drama, and affording new satisfaction to the audience.

In every detail of performance a singing actress is dependent on the singers who play opposite her. I have never understood the star who enjoys playing with a mediocre cast in order to shine out the more brilliantly himself, for the essence of any fine dramatic or operatic production is harmonious integration of all performances. Alfred Jerger, with whom I sang in Strauss' *Intermezzo* and *Arabella*, and the unforgettable Richard Mayr, furnished perfect complements to my acting efforts, I found. I will never forget our *Rosenkavalier* rehearsals in which Mayr, playing the part of Baron Ochs, struck the keynote of the whole performance for me in his vivid characterization. Stage association with other inspiring actors is a stimulation for one's own performance that cannot be measured. The final integration of the work of one actor with another comes, of course, through the stage director.

We have come to realize the close integration between all aspects of opera, to know that neither music nor action, nor staging, is sufficient unto itself, or unto an operatic production as a whole. A practical and effective stage director will not attempt to force his ideas on an actress, nor will a sensitive interpreter persist in a portrayal which does not jibe with the rest of the production. There must always be give and take between stage director and singing actor or actress, to bring two dissimilar interpretations into a satisfactory dramatic balance. Most conductors concern themselves solely with the music, but there are exceptions. Toscanini and Bruno Walter, for example, have an eye for the stage as well as the music, and with such men as these one hardly needs a regisseur.

I shall always remember with gratitude the man to whom I owe the original decision to attempt *Fidelio*. It was on the occasion of the Beethoven Centenary in 1926 that Franz Schalk inspired me to try this. I trusted his friendly advice and can never forget his interpretation of this noblest of all operas, his humble, wholly forgetful musicianship, and — I may rightly be proud to say it — his joy in my Leonora. I have since sung the role under various conductors, but I shall always remember most fondly Franz Schalk to whom I owe Leonora, Bruno Walter who led me to a deeper conception of the part, and Arturo Toscanini who raised me above myself with his strong, suggestive will. Schalk, if he liked a voice very much, was apt to forget in his enthusiasm that there are limits to a singer's powers. Walter, on the contrary, was careful always to eliminate the element of strain. His deep understanding and great sympathy for the singer are perhaps not to be equaled. The artist is continually protected by his consideration, and technical difficulties of singing and nervous inhibitions alike are easily overcome under such a conductor. When first I sang opera under the inexorable Toscanini I was a little apprehensive. One hears everywhere of Toscanini's inspiring rehearsals, but also a good deal about his lack of consideration. I had even heard that he required ten hours a day of singing with full voice. (My hair stood on end at this thought.) Actually Toscanini was full of consideration, always advising us to save our voices when, under the spell of his magic, we spent ourselves too lavishly. One thing, to be sure, he demanded: concentration — unconditional devotion to the task in hand and complete, perfect understanding of its scope. But no true artist could possibly remain passive in the presence of this passionate, almost fanatic will. Toscanini knows no concessions, he despises all incompetence, and where Walter overcame difficulties with understanding and sympathy, it was Toscanini's glowing will that wrought perfection. It is an overpowering force that would impel one to follow him even if the Maestro's own selfless devotion to his work did not immediately rule out anything but uninterrupted concentration on the part of the musicians under him.

It may be of interest to the reader to know something of the rehearsal procedure for a new opera. After thoroughly studying the libretto and music by himself the singer has several rehearsals with the co-repetitor. It is

the co-repetitor who assists the conductor at all rehearsals and often conducts the singers from the prompt-
box at a performance, so that the conductor can give
more attention to the orchestra. When he has thoroughly mastered the part, the singer goes over it with
the conductor at the piano for several rehearsals. Then
follow more rehearsals with the other singers, but without chorus. These rehearsals take place on the stage
with the co-repetitor at the piano and under the direction of the regisseur. During stage rehearsals the regisseur makes constant suggestions, since he sees the stage
as a whole, which of course the singer is not able to do.
The regisseur is, as it were, the mirror in which the
unified production is reflected. Next come rehearsals
with chorus, and, finally, with the orchestra. It is important to note that there is never a rehearsal without
music, and that the action is never disassociated from
the musical background.

The physical means of projecting a characterization
in opera — the gesture and movement — are, of course,
affected not only by the scale of the music but (just as a
dramatic performance would be) by the scenic production and the size of the stage and auditorium.

Where there may be three or twenty-three theatres
in a large city, there is rarely more than one opera
house. The opera auditorium must, therefore, be large
enough to accommodate a goodly audience at one time.
Then, too, where the theatre stage may be intimately

proportioned for drawing-room comedy with a small cast of characters, operatic stages must be large enough to accommodate huge choruses.

Wagner was the first composer to take the size of the opera house into consideration and to write operas of broad universal theme to which the sweeping and elemental gesture (which the size of the opera house demands) is far more suited than is the minute and intimate gesture of the small stage. Perhaps the reason that the public recognizes a tradition of convincing operatic acting in the Wagner operas is because of their very adaptability to the large operatic stage. The old Italian and French operas, on the other hand, with their small-scale action, have had to be over-acted on the big opera stages, in order to be projected across the footlights at all; and so an audience, accustomed to fine nuances of acting on the legitimate stage, is often apt to think of the opera singer as over-playing his role.

Dr. Herbert Graf's Philadelphia production of *Der Rosenkavalier* several years ago, in which the stage was cut down to proportions suited to the action of the boudoir and tavern scenes, which are on small comedy scale, enabled the opera actors to play the opera with a new respect for its subtle comedy values. The reverse problem presented itself to Dr. Graf at Salzburg, however. There it was found necessary to enlarge a very small opera stage. Dr. Graf did an extraordinary job with the tiny Salzburg Festival stage in putting on the

LOTTE LEHMANN
in *Der Rosenkavalier*

LOTTE LEHMANN
in *Manon*

mob scene and the final festival scene in *Die Meister-
singer*. In each case he had two-hundred-and-twenty-five
people on a tiny stage, and, since he could not fit them
gracefully on one level, he built up various levels, ac-
commodating three times as many people as would have
been possible otherwise.

Whatever questions of technique and problems of production may precede the operatic performance, it has
been my own experience that in the instant of the actual
singing of an opera role we are apt to forget all techni-
calities. When I am giving myself over completely to
any part, I do not have time to analyze my approach or
attack. I am afraid I play the part only as I know in my
heart that it *must* be done, unconsciously echoing
Mephisto's advice to Faust in Goethe's illuminating
lines:

> *Grau, teuerer Freund, ist alle Theorie —*
> *Und grün des Lebens gold'ner Baum.*
>
> *(All theory, dear friend, is drab —*
> *And fresh the golden tree of life.)*